A Consumer's Guide to Information

How to Avoid Losing Your Mind on the Internet

Katherine Pickering Antonova

Copyright © 2016 Katherine M. Antonova

All Rights Reserved

ISBN 978-1-5201-7988-9

This is for Anya and Marina:
in the hope that your generation handles information
better than your elders have.

Contents

Chapter One

Information Revolution

In the early stages of the industrial revolution, people reported being terrified or nauseated by the speed of the new trains, and changes in work and the environment massively altered most people's lives, often in ways that were deeply damaging. Today we are living in the early stages of an information revolution that is similarly transforming most aspects of our lives, and it can be overwhelming.

This Is Hard for Everybody

We have easy access to enormous amounts of information, but it has also become harder to escape the bombardment. While it should be easier than ever to find out what we need to know, in some ways this too has actually become harder, because there is so much unhelpful information to sort through first.

Moreover, our own brains are fighting us. We are not built to manage information at the speeds we now confront. The constant distraction caused by alerts and alarms emanating from our personal devices makes it difficult to focus. Staring at lighted screens after dark disrupts our sleep. And more deeply, various defense mechanisms that humans have developed to cope with risk and threats in the physical world can actually make us more vulnerable in the digital world, where we get the wrong information, miss what we do need, and get manipulated or cheated by those who use our vulnerability for their gain.

The onslaught of information we face every waking minute of the day is not just hard on our minds and bodies and a source of vulnerability. Too much information often just makes us feel bad. We are exposed to a great deal of sad or difficult news even when it doesn't affect us. We are pressured to make decisions without being able to master what's at stake in them. We know so much about each other that we are often battling feelings of jealousy, hurt, fear, and worry about how we stand in relation to others, what they think of us, and how different many of us really are, even while most people actually get along just fine with others in face-to-face encounters.

It is tempting to just turn away from this upsetting wall of noise. However, the interconnectedness of our world through information is now so dense that total avoidance is impossible. This book offers basic critical thinking strategies to help anyone navigate the minefield of non-stop information. If we were all a little better at handling the situation, the situation would improve for everyone.

How to Use This Book

This book is for anyone who feels overwhelmed by information in general or stressed by the difficulty of finding what we need and can rely on, in particular. These days that might well be all of us.

Casual readers who are looking to improve their approach to information in certain realms should feel free to jump around: the subheadings in each chapter are meant to make the book easy to navigate.

Those who are just beginning to think about how they consume information should find plenty to ponder by simply reading through from beginning to end.

Those who want to do serious work on becoming a savvy citizen in the world of digital information are recommended to skim the book first for an overview, and then move slowly section by section, trying out the ideas here one at a time, with frequent breaks.

Improving our information literacy is hard work that takes time, but like most skills it gets faster and more automatic with practice, and comes with a big payoff. In this case, the payoff will be getting reliable answers to our questions, knowing how to avoid being manipulated or conned, and having the confidence of being able to defend our views and the security of knowing we are acting on solid information.

What Is Critical Thinking?

Critical thinking is not a negative approach to the world. Critical thinking is a rational process of sorting and weighing information so that we can find what we need and have confidence in what we know.

It is a way of training our brains to overcome those instincts that work against us in the world of information. It is also a way of seeing the world beyond our personal perspective. It shows us how our actions affect others we haven't met. This teaches us how to act with compassion and fairness not just toward the people we meet face-to-face, but toward all those whose lives we touch.

Can You Handle the Truth?

Critical thinking is an active, effortful practice. Especially at the beginning, if it hurts it means you're doing it right, much like a physical workout. We have to train ourselves to work past our first reactions, because these reactions tend to be not just emotional, but specifically grounded in the feelings of our "lizard brain," where fear, disgust, panic and other extreme reactions are triggered before we have a full understanding of our situation.

Even people who have many years of training and experience in research fields still need to constantly remind themselves to question their own biases and go through mental checklists, though other parts of the critical thinking process become second nature with time.

Paying Attention

Critical thinking is also more than a set of skills that we can practice. It requires a degree of mindful attention that is more difficult to find time for now than ever. Think of mindful attention as the kind of zone an artist or athlete gets into at their best.

For example, ordinarily when we look at someone's face, our brains rush to recognize the person and read their expression, because that's what we need to do most of the time. But we can make a conscious effort to look at that face in a completely different way, as an artist does, seeing details we normally gloss over like the fact that the face takes up the bottom part of the head only, or the way shadows contour the features.

This willful act of shifting focus and noticing what you didn't see on first glance is also central to critical thinking.

Engaging with Ideas

To engage with ideas means to try them out, understand them, and walk around with them awhile without judging them. Judging may follow, but the only way to truly disagree with an idea—to do so with certainty, in a way you can defend to others—is to first fully understand it from the perspective of those who hold the idea. You have to temporarily let your own certainties, expectations, and experiences be set aside in order to take in another view of the world. Then you return to your own, hopefully having been enriched by your journey.

This is not a comfortable process. If you're doing it right, it should fill you with doubt, and maybe even guilt, shame, fear, and anger. This is because you need to seriously entertain a reality where what you think you know is not, in fact, true. That is an upsetting sensation. When you're done with this process you might come back to where you began, or you might come back somewhere nearly where you began, or perhaps you'll land somewhere unexpected. You can't know, or the process won't work.

Entertaining real uncertainty and doubt is incredibly difficult. It is a leap of faith, where you unmoor yourself from much of what you know—and therefore from much of yourself—and imagine a different, unfamiliar world that feels alien and perhaps unwelcoming (at least at first). In order to land in a place of confidence and enlightenment, you have to rely on the process. It is like stepping into a dark space, but doing so knowing that there is solid ground under your feet even when you can't see what it looks like. The ground beneath your feet is made of evidence and reasoning. This is what supports our explorations of the outside world.

Confronting Disappointment

This process may also lead you to realize that a source you have trusted in the past has misled you. To avoid feeling that betrayal of trust or out of loyalty to people we respect we are sometimes tempted to gloss over such incidents as insignificant exceptions.

Critical thinking requires, though, that we determine what caused our source to feed us unreliable information, so we can make a reasoned decision about whether we can continue to rely on that source. Sometimes the most trusted sources will mislead us by accident. Sources with the best intentions may mislead us out of ignorance or confusion.

You can acknowledge good intentions without accepting the misleading conclusions your source came to. You can be more loyal in the long run by not enabling people you respect to continue to be misled and to mislead others.

Don't First Look at the Source

The first mistake most people make when trying to assess the value of information is to rely on where the information came from: who said it? What's your source?

In fact, you'll often see this as the first piece of advice in many free online guides to spotting "fake" information. One of the problems with this advice is that it just reinforces divisions when people already only trust information from their own "side," and are therefore predisposed to reject anything from alternative sources on principle.

But information, facts, truth, and reality itself do not have sides, and that's the stuff we're looking for. The biggest problem with the advice to "look at the source" is simply that the source really doesn't matter very much. This mistake is known as the "appeal to authority fallacy." This fallacy says that because someone said X, if we respect or like or trust that someone as an authority, then what they say must be true. That's bad logic because anyone can be wrong, whether because they're lying, don't know better, or they simply made a mistake or don't have the appropriate information or experience in this particular case.

Follow the Evidence

So what else do we have to go on? The golden rule at the core of all critical thinking is: follow the evidence. If a source is really worth listening to, they will show you their evidence and explain their reasoning about it so you can judge it for yourself.

When you read a claim someone makes, look for what evidence they share and how they explain they arrived at their conclusions, and ask yourself what they left out, long before considering who said it.

What Evidence Means: Reasoning

Alongside evidence, we look for reasoning that links the evidence to claims. In other words, when we evaluate how reliable or useful a piece of information is, we look for data, documentation, testimony, etc., we weigh that evidence, and we also assess the logic and plausibility of how that evidence is supposed to support the conclusion we're interested in. This process together is what critical thinking is all about. It will become clearer as we look at examples.

Your Brain Is a Traitor

There are several ways our brains make it harder for us to process information accurately that we should learn to recognize as we feel them happen, though their names are not important:

Confirmation Bias – We are tribal creatures who value belonging and bonding with others like ourselves. We are predisposed to recognize and believe whatever information confirms what we've already chosen to agree or identify with. This can make us miss vital new information, or problems with what we think we already know.

The Dunning-Kruger Effect – When we know little about a subject, we're actually more likely to feel certain of our opinions about it, and to rate ourselves as experts. Learning more about the subject teaches us how much more there is to know, and leads to more tentative, yet actually sounder, conclusions. This is a dangerous problem, because not having information we need makes us vulnerable, yet we actually double-down on false or limited conclusions and aggressively reject that which challenges them, putting ourselves even more at risk.

Cognitive Dissonance – So that we may survive the many contradictory streams of information and experience hitting us every day, we often accept a principle in one aspect of our lives while arguing against it in another, without noticing the contradiction. It is a defense mechanism to avoid confronting our most difficult problems. But the cost of this tendency is that we behave like hypocrites, not even living up to our own values in some aspects of our lives.

False Equivalence – Our minds seek balance and fairness, and this is reinforced at tremendous volume by a media environment that emphasizes presenting two sides to everything rather than doing the more difficult work of fact-checking and researching multiple perspectives. So we tell ourselves that we are fair and objective when we politely acknowledge "both" sides on any question, or decide to "agree to disagree." In reality, however, any issue worth discussing has more than two sides, and the evidence probably does not shake out equally among all of them. Truthfulness is more important than neutrality. We need to know the truth so that our choices really fit our values and needs.

Correspondence Bias – We usually understand how our own mistakes are partly due to extenuating circumstances, but we tend to judge other people's mistakes as solely the result of their inherent character. This is closely related to our tendency to pay more attention to things that irritate or threaten us than to things that help us. The sad result is that we often take just one incident or fact as defining whole people or groups, especially when what little we know is negative.

Selective Memory and Attention – The reason things like astrology or fortune-telling can seem spookily accurate is that we notice and remember facts that confirm the idea, while not noticing or dismissing as irrelevant anything that contradicts it. This function is how our brains sort through the non-stop input from our environments to focus on what we need to know, but it can play tricks on us. Instead of needing to remember which characteristics mark a path that leads back to water, we now need to sort through much more complex and sometimes deliberately deceptive clues to understand abstract concepts, and to do that well we have to make more conscious choices about where to focus our attention.

Illusory Truth Effect – One of the ways we manage being constantly confronted with new information is that we start taking repeated information for granted, so that we can focus on new input. One of the costs of this trait, though, is that when we read or hear the same false statement over and over—even if we know from the start that it's untrue—we begin to believe it without realizing what we're doing. The more we see the false statement, the more we believe it, and we can even reach a point where we will dig our heels and defend the false statement when it's debunked, just because it has become part of our mental landscape through repetition. Note how this makes us frighteningly easy to manipulate!

Questioning Ourselves

The following questions are a guide we can walk ourselves through to help us set aside our assumptions, biases, and blind spots in order to engage with ideas critically. We should ask ourselves these questions deeply, with careful thought about each one, and we should remind ourselves of these questions each time we approach a situation when we confront a really difficult problem or disagreement.

1. Is it possible that I am sometimes wrong? (Of course it is.)

2. Are there things I don't know? (Of course there are.)

3. Is it possible that other people know things I don't, and could tell me things that are to my advantage? (Of course it is.)

4. If someone I trust says something, does that make it true? (No, it doesn't.)

5. My perspective is valid and real. Are other people's perspectives also valid and real? (Of course they are.)

6. Do I know what other people's perspectives actually are without listening to them? (Of course I don't.)

7. What specific harm will result from listening to a different perspective with an open mind and heart? (None: listening is free and safe.)

8. On subjects where I feel certain I'm right, what is the source of my certainty? (Is my knowledge comprehensive, vetted by myself and other experts, and still subject to new evidence? Is it up-to-date?)

9. If a statement makes me feel strong emotions, do my feelings make that statement true or untrue? (Of course they don't.)

10. Are my feelings more important than the truth? (If I am the only person affected, that's my call. But if other people are affected, I can't deliberately avoid truth just to spare my feelings.)

11. How does it make me feel to consider listening to contrary opinions with an open mind? How do I feel while actually listening? What are those feelings trying to tell me? Can I let them wash over me and wait to see what's on the other side? (Yes, I can.)

12. I am entitled to my opinion, but is my opinion worth sharing? (Is it based in truth about the world, beyond my personal feelings? Does it add something productive to a discussion?)

When Evidence and Reasoning Won't Help

Some subjects or questions are knowable, and some are not. Empirical data and rational analysis can't solve every problem or answer every question. There are many important spheres of life where critical thinking cannot help us.

But we also need to acknowledge those areas where not knowing and not thinking cost us dearly. We do not need to leap to indulge our outrage, fear, disgust, contempt, anger, or desires without first confirming that these feelings are grounded in reality and assessing how we can respond to them in a productive way. We can avoid leaping to conclusions without evidence, and we can remind ourselves to handle information especially carefully just when it seems to feed our deepest fears or desires. That is precisely the moment, when much is at stake, that we owe it to ourselves to be sure of our facts.

Chapter Two

What's the Good News?

One of the most dangerous and unpleasant realities of internet media today is the pervasive presence of fake news that is intended to manipulate our views or take our money. Deliberately manipulated "news" is far worse than the mistakes or ill-advised reporting we sometimes see from legitimate news sources, much less the occasional questionable editorial choice or minor error—quickly corrected—from the most reputable news organizations, which get that reputation by relying on journalists with professional training (including in ethics), fact-checking their work, and then having it further evaluate by editors.

Tabloids Have Invaded Your Home

The manipulation of information is as old as time. But before the internet, most fake news aimed at the public was relegated to tabloids at the supermarket checkout, and that physical context gave us clues about how trustworthy that information might be. But today when nearly all information reaches us as words on a screen, we have far fewer clues to distinguish one type from another. Often we see news when it is shared with us by friends in a social media space that feels personal, and that makes us tend to give it more trust than we would if we encountered it at random in a public space. And because of the ease and cheapness of today's software, anyone can produce what looks like real news articles, except that they completely invent the content out of thin air. The process of making fakes is so easy, and the means of bringing it to us so misleading, that most of us, no matter how savvy and whatever our views, have been taken in by fake news at some point.

Viral Lies

Because Americans increasingly get and share their news on social media platforms, these fake news articles can go viral, being seen and believed by millions around the world, long before anyone can begin to refute them. Debunking such articles takes time, but the results are also less dramatic, and don't get shared as often. Even after reading that a piece of news was debunked, many people remember only the fake version just a short time later.

The Con

Reporting just before the 2016 U.S. Presidential election, Buzzfeed found more than 100 fake news sites run from a single town in Macedonia. The sites were made purely to profit from advertising, and they experimented with fake news supporting candidates from both parties.

Profit is often the motivation for producing fakes, but sometimes they are purposefully intended to sway our political views, made by people with vested interests in the outcome of an election.

The Joke

Other forms of fake news are made just to be funny, and such sites should reveal themselves as "satirical" somewhere, but this information might be in small print, or not noticeable from the headline shared on social media. The Onion is the most well-known of these, and others include the "Borowitz Report" in The New Yorker, Sports Pickle, Private Eye (a UK version of The Onion), News Biscuit, Unconfirmed Sources, and CAP News (which imitates the ABC News logo).

Fake News Is Making Us Miserable

Other than satire sites, fake news is usually made to be intentionally disturbing, often presenting horrifying details that make ordinary people question the decency of the world. That's what gets attention, and therefore the clicks that result in advertising money. The cumulative result of seeing a lot of this kind of fake news, however, is depression, anxiety, and fear—all of it unnecessary, since these horrible events never occurred. There's enough real bad news in the world already. Let's not allow ourselves to be upset by the fake stuff.

Headlines to Stop Clicking On

The first step when assessing whether a news story is fake is to notice whether the headline you see is playing to your emotions. Fake news headlines are often either extremely vivid and shocking ("Mother kills baby with a hatchet, then eats puppies!") or full of vivid language with no details, forcing you to click to the site to find out what the headline refers to ("Obama DESTROYED Warren with this comment"). Another common tactic is for the snappy headline to contradict a dominant media narrative (during a week of news about school shootings, a headline saying: "Ninja principal tackles shooter and prevents tragedy!"). These kinds of headlines feed a wish in our minds to not have to accept what the real news is telling us lately. Finally, headlines that pose a question ("Did Adele Really Pose Naked with a Monkey?") can usually be answered with a simple "no" without even bothering to click through. Framing a claim as a question is a sneaky way to pretend you're not spreading something you know is false.

One solid strategy for remaining sane is to simply not click on any such headlines. The chances of them being true, or truly interesting, are minimal. If you're curious, search Twitter for accounts that "spoil" "click bait" news. These accounts read the article for you and tweet the key information missing from the headline (they tend not to last long, probably because the task is herculean). Just reading some of these twitter feeds, such as @BaitClickSpoilr and @ClickBaitSpoilr, is an entertaining look at how manipulative those headlines really are. Along similar lines, follow journalist @ CraigSilverman for frequent call-outs of fake news as well as errors in mainstream media.

Another quick way to avoid clicking on sketchy headlines is to skim the comments on the post first—if the news is fake, often someone will have pointed this out by the time you see it, and save you some trouble.

The Trickiest Fakes

But some forms of fake news work harder to trick you. These headlines are shocking or disturbing, but the language isn't so hyped up, so that it might still sound like a real news site (especially since real news organizations are starting to write headlines in the same terrible way to compete for our clicks).

Some fakers use site names that are intended to be mistaken for a real local newspaper, like The Denver Guardian. Others use web addresses that begin the same way as major networks, like "www.abc.com.co". Always look at the URL (Universal Resource Locator—the address for any website—located in the address bar at the top of your browser) to confirm that you really are looking at what you think you are.

Most established US websites end in .com, .org, .net, .gov, or .edu, and usually the part of the address before that ending is just the company or institution name. Be suspicious of misspellings, extra components, unusual endings, or strange names in a web address. That said, some "strange" endings for a US viewer may be a standard ending for another country, such as ".mx" for Mexico or ".no" for Norway. British commercial websites end in ".co.uk," which should not be confused with just ".co".

To be on the safe side, just do an independent search for the organization's name, which should quickly bring up the official site (usually designated as such in the search results).

How to Not Get Conned

The best strategy to spot fake news is to get independent confirmation of the key facts, or to identify inconsistencies that suggest the information was manipulated. None of these steps is difficult or time-consuming, but you may have to go through several of them before you're sure of what you're looking at.

Check the Date

Sometimes old stories are recycled and shared (often by accident) as if they're current. The same story can be shared over and over, sometimes with a few details or the picture changed, to give an impression that some event is a constant phenomenon when it actually happened only once.

Who Started It?

Do a quick general internet search to see if the website the story comes from is actually a news organization.

If the story comes from a blog, you'll have to dig a bit further. Often blogs make small, local news stories go viral by sharing and discussing them, but a legitimate blog should link you back to the source of the story on a legitimate news site or official report from the appropriate authority. Occasionally a blogger will break a real news story, but that is only possible if that blogger has direct access to events or people who make news. If that is the case, the blogger should explain how he was the first person to make the event or statement public, and those facts should be documented or confirmed by independent authorities before we rely on it.

Sometimes a report comes through a news site specializing in opinion and analysis like Slate or The Weekly Standard that does little or no original reporting, and these sites may link you back still further. If a story is legitimate, you should be able to trace it back through links to a news organization with reporters in the location where the story occurred, or to official police or government reports.

Be suspicious of vague reports that say "according to police" or "according to local news sources" without actually naming or linking them. That's an easy way to make something sound official when it isn't.

Often a legitimate local news organization will be named, but when you search its site, there's no mention of the viral story. That suggests it didn't happen. Other times, when you search for the local newspaper or TV station that is named as reporting the story, there is no such newspaper or TV station, though the name will often be suspiciously similar to a real one.

Where Did It Happen?

You can also search the location where a news story is said to have happened to find out what the major newspapers and stations are, then go straight to those local news sites to see if they're reporting on the same event. If they're not, again it's likely that the story was fake.

In some cases you can search Twitter for the emergency (police, fire, and EMT) scanners for the relevant location. Major crimes would be noted in this way, though not every location has twitter feeds for emergency scanners.

Look for Quotes

Is anyone quoted in the article? Many fake news sites quote unnamed "witnesses" or "officials" and that's a dead giveaway—legitimate news sources attribute quotes to the speaker (only a few national papers regularly allow high-level government sources to be quoted anonymously by reporters who meet with them personally and stake their own reputations on the quotes being real).

When an official is quoted, do a quick google search of the quote to see if it was recorded on video or in a transcript on a legitimate site, such as a major, respected news organization or a government body. The statements of important elected officials are constantly recorded by multiple parties: if you don't find the full quote with context recorded somewhere with unassailable legitimacy, you should assume it didn't happen.

When you do find a quote confirmed somewhere, look to see whether there's more context available, including not only what was said before and after the quote, but where it was said, to what audience, and for what purpose.

"The Lamestream Media Won't Cover This!"

News is often shared on social media with a sarcastic comment about how the mainstream media refuses to cover it. It's true that the digital revolution can give us access to important information we can't otherwise get, without editorial filters telling us what we should know. The mainstream media does have a recognized tendency to underreport foreign news, and the kinds of crimes or tragedies that are sadly common but not considered exciting enough to bring in the views and clicks that news organizations depend on for funding. However, one other reason stories don't make it into the mainstream media is simply that reporters looked into it and didn't find anything that could be verified. Be especially careful with stories that aren't getting any attention from established press organizations.

Altered Images

If a suspicious news story comes with images, the first thing to do is to see if the image was digitally altered in ways we can spot. Shadows and light sources should be consistent through all parts of the photo, and people's limbs should all have natural angles.

A classic trick is to show someone holding a sign with something shocking written on it, because it's very easy to erase the words on a sign and type in your own using photo manipulation software.

Next, if there are multiple images or different images in different versions of the story, check that they match. Do the people, objects, and background scenery or buildings look like the same location in each photograph? It's very common for an image from a previous or related but much less dramatic incident to be used to lend weight to a fake story. Is a picture of a group of people surrounding a vehicle about a riot, a traffic incident, or a popular food truck? Are the people in the photo fighting, helping, or just curious? When a headline tells us what's happening, we project appropriate actions and intentions onto the people in the photograph. When the headline is invented, we can walk away thinking we've seen "proof" through this completely faulty mechanism.

In the same way, separate the caption from the image. Often an image that is confusing or open to interpretation is manipulated by a firmly worded caption to seem to depict much more than it really does. Try imagining a completely different caption for the image to see if it, too, could be just as plausible with this image.

You can also check whether an image really depicts what it's supposed to depict by capturing a screenshot and dragging it into Google Images. The search will find similar images from all over the internet, including what might be (other) fakes. But if you read the sites linked there for background information, you may be able to detect the original source of the image.

But Video Is Proof, Right? (Nope)

Video is harder to fake, but still can't be trusted automatically. The audio track is the easiest thing to add or subtract from a video, and bits of someone's speech can be edited into a new order by anyone on a laptop with fairly basic software. Video images that are dark, blurry, or otherwise hard to make out can be manipulated with faked audio to appeal to your senses and make you feel like you're seeing a lot more than you actually are. Try watching it with the sound muted (or listen to just the audio and look at something else). Video can also be taken out of context, either by editing out crucial portions or taking video from one incident and claiming it is something else altogether.

What This Meme Needs Is a Cat

One further way that fake news gets circulated is through memes. Memes are viral images that usually present a brief, supposedly factual claim superimposed over a disturbing or famous photo.

First remember that the photo and text were put together for effect, but are not necessarily connected at all. When a person is photographed often enough there's a complete catalog of expressions available to illustrate anything we like. This is how we can get a photo of a movie star making a face after sipping too-hot coffee used to illustrate a bland statement made in a discussion about a fictional character labeled as an "attack" on a supposed "rival" or former romantic attachment, even though neither the photo nor the statement had anything to do with that person.

Quotes by famous people are very easy to fake, but also easy to check. If you search the key words of the quote you will probably find out quickly who said it, although be careful with search results that just lead you back to the same false meme, or another inaccurate attribution. Use Chapter 3 to help you identify reliable sources.

Memes that show data or claim some famous person did something great or terrible are also incredibly easy to fake. You can say George Washington just landed on the moon if you want to, but that doesn't make it true. It takes only a moment to independently verify what the meme is telling you. Memes from reliable sources will put the source of their claims in small print somewhere on the image. Look up that website or organization (independently searching its name, not following the given address directly) and see if what they say on their own website matches what's on the meme. See also Chapter 6.

When You Don't Have the Time

Another, quicker method to check whether a story is fake is to look it up on a number of sites that do the kind of checking described above for you. For viral stories of all kinds, Snopes.com is the most respected site (there's a fake news story going around about its CEO being arrested, but that's…fake). Others specializing in revealing hoaxes include TruthorFiction.com and HoaxSlayer.com. GossipCop.com specializes in fact-checking stories about celebrities. These sites should explain the basis of their evaluation of any claim or hoax so you can judge for yourself, so be sure to read their whole explanation, not just the verdict.

One list of sites with a documented history of producing fake news or news satire was quickly removed due to threats against its creator, which should tell us a great deal about how much people profit from deceiving the public and what lengths they will go to to keep that deception alive. Other lists are still available, and are especially reliable when composed by the websites that specialize in tracking hoaxes. There are also browser extensions such as "BS Detector" for Chrome that will alert you when you have landed on a site that shows characteristics consistent with fake news. Facebook has recently announced that it will be implementing a similar feature to identify suspect articles.

Breaking News

Another form of news that often turns out to be false are the very early reports coming from even legitimate news organizations in the aftermath of a major event. Before 24-hour cable news and the internet, people heard little more than the fact that a major event had occurred until some hours or even a day later, by which time professional journalists would have had time to separate rumors from official reports. But today news organizations are under pressure to inform us fully even in the moment that events are occurring. They often give in to rumors and guesswork, and even official reports can be confused in the early hours. The best strategy is simply to turn off the news and give it a day or two to sort itself out.

What if We Can't Wait?

But sometimes we can't or don't want to wait for clarity to assert itself. In that case, the most reliable reports will be the most local ones, and preferably from official sources like police departments. Emergency scanner Twitter feeds or other local official Twitter accounts are a place to start. Sometimes eyewitnesses to an event will tweet photos or comments, but remember that each individual's perspective is limited to what they can see and hear—they cannot give you a full picture.

You can also search for the local newspapers or TV affiliates, and go directly to their websites. These organizations have reporters nearby who know local conditions, and they are most likely to have an accurate idea of the situation and to not want to unduly panic local residents.

The Lamestream Media?

Professional journalists do, of course, make mistakes, especially during live reporting of ongoing events. The best and most reliable organizations will correct these mistakes on air or in print as soon as possible. Seeing such corrections is a good sign that you're dealing with reliable professionals (though not a guarantee).

Getting Real News

The first step to find out whether your usual news sources are reliable is to search their website and look them up on Wikipedia for information about their staff and methods. High-quality news outlets pay professional journalists, researchers, and fact-checkers. They have reporters on the ground in relevant locations to get first-hand reports. Their editors should have long experience and relevant educational backgrounds.

Supporting the Good Stuff

High-quality reporting is expensive and slower than being careless, so when you find a good source of news, consider supporting it financially by subscribing or donating, because free internet media has endangered the ability of these professionals to do their work. That endangers us all when fake news is so prevalent. Remember that websites that provide news analysis and opinion rely on the original reporting from traditional organizations like Reuters, the Associated Press, The Washington Post, The New York Times, The Wall Street Journal, The Boston Globe, The Chicago Tribune, and other longstanding regional papers, and can't exist without them.

By the same token, when you see news organizations behaving irresponsibly, avoid clicking or sharing the item, and instead write to the editors to point out the problem. If you feel the "mainstream media" is doing a poor job, tell them what you want instead, giving specific examples directed toward the news organizations that most bother you.

When you see ads from companies you do business with supporting news sites that behave irresponsibly, contact those companies to let them know what they're supporting (internet advertising is often purchased in bundles and companies may not know which specific sites their ads appear on). Follow and support MediaMatters.org, which is an independent watchdog organization for newsmedia.

Why Is News So Awful, Anyway?

Until about twenty or thirty years ago network TV news divisions ran at a loss, which was easily offset by their much larger entertainment divisions. Networks were happy enough with this situation, since the news divisions lent prestige and satisfied Congressional and FCC requirements about public-service broadcasting.

This began to change, though, as cable entertainment and other new technologies, from VCRs to the internet and streaming entertainment, cut away at network profits, and then print newspaper profits as well. Networks began to demand that news divisions make a profit to carry their weight, and some newspapers and news magazines folded or shrunk while others increasingly pandered to specific audiences to keep people loyal enough to subscribe. At the same time, USA Today brought touches of television's flashiness to newspapers with success, pushing others to move the same way. The quality and tone of American news changed radically.

Because they profit from their reports according to how many eyeballs they attract, news producers now emphasize drama, play to our emotions—especially fear, which provokes the quickest and most vivid response—and try to make every conversation seem like a fight. These influences have sadly deteriorated the quality of news, but also arguably deteriorated the quality of life for all of us, as well as undermining our ability to base our decisions about policy and politics on reality.

Another part of the problem is that 24-hour cable news networks not only have to turn a profit, they have to fight for our attention all day and night, so that they put even more energy into milking our credibility and emotions.

Finally, since the Fox News channel first showed how very lucrative slanted news can be, it became common for some cable news channels to play overtly to specific audiences, emphasizing stories and angles that deliberately increase divisiveness among Americans. Others use false equivalence to showcase the most extreme views as if they are much more popular or legitimate than they are, in order to shock and worry us into watching them more.

If you have the opportunity to watch television news from a country where news divisions are non-profit, or our own news networks from before about 1990 (on YouTube) you'll find that it is much more boring, more reliable, and less dangerous and upsetting than what we are used to today.

Getting Independent Confirmation

Another way to approach judging the overall reliability of a newspaper or TV outlet is to experiment with independently confirming some of its stories.

Look up the same story on several other, non-tabloid news websites. Don't just look for one known for having the opposite point of view. Find a variety of perspectives, and look at different ones each time. Look at sites with an out-of-the-ordinary take like The Conversation, The Intercept, Alt-M (altmuslimah.com) or Foreign Affairs and sites known primarily for analysis like The Economist, Forbes, The Atlantic, and The New Republic as well as outlets that do their own reporting. Try newspapers and magazines known for in-depth, long-form investigations like Mother Jones or The Christian Science Monitor. Compare The Weekly Standard to The Nation.

For news that's important enough to get international coverage, compare American news with the BBC (UK), the CBC or CTV (Canada), ABC (Australia), DW (Germany), France24, Radio France Internationale, Al Jazeera English, The Independent, The Guardian, The Financial Times, The West Australian, Spiegel Online International, or Le Monde diplomatique English Edition, which can all be accessed online at least partially without a subscription.

If you can read other languages, you may have access to more, but many countries also publish some English-language news, usually intended for expatriates living in those countries. If you search "English news Russia," for example, you will find The Moscow Times as well as the RT television network, and if you search "English news Japan" you get Japan Today and The Japan Times. You can also consult Wikipedia's "Lists of newspapers by country," which sometimes specifies the papers that are published in English, and often indicates their circulation numbers and known political slants. Just the beginning of what you can get online in English includes: The Rio Times, NewsinEnglish.no (Norway), TheLocal.se (Sweden), The Straits Times (Singapore), Today Venezuela, Mexico News Daily and TheNews.mx (Mexico), and The South China Morning Post. Much of the coverage in these sources will be domestic or regional, but it can be instructive to see how differently domestic news is reported around the world.

Finally, take a look at newseum.org to compare front pages from around the world at a glance.

Finding the Evidence

When reading specific stories, as always look first for evidence. Does the report leap to an explanation of why someone is doing something without showing how they know? That would be a bad sign. Does the report rely on statistics, polls, or surveys? See Chapter 6 on how to approach this kind of evidence. Does the report quote witnesses or experts? Search the key words of the quote and the person's name, and see whether other outlets provided more context for it or quoted it more completely. Look into who the witness or expert is, and whether they have the access or knowledge to speak definitively on the subject of the quotation.

Facts versus Opinion

In the middle and later parts of the twentieth century, standard newspaper-style reporting was supposed to be "just the facts." Articles would open with "who what when where" and the rest of the piece would explain further details and context about what happened, but not try to make a case about "why" an event occurred or tell you what to conclude from it. Editorial opinions and commentary were kept in an obviously separate section and labeled as such. The known political "slants" of given newspapers were expected to be specific to their editorials pages and not be reflected in the straight news reporting, according to the journalistic ethics that developed as part of the professionalization of journalism in the last century and more.

Today, however, online and television journalism increasingly blur the lines between news reporting and opinion. The best way to be aware of which you're reading or listening to is to pay attention to how the writer or speaker presents what happened: concrete actions and events described as "reported by Chief of Police So-and-So" or "according to such-and-such witness" are more reliable than qualified statements like "it seems that…" or "one would think…" or "people are saying…" or any explanations of the larger meanings of a given event.

Talking Heads

When two people of opposing views are brought on TV to discuss a topic, that usually means they have nothing other than opposing views to present. You are unlikely to learn new facts from them, and whatever facts are presented by the speakers are manipulated by that format into appearing to be of equal weight, whether they really are or not.

The people invited to speak in those segments vary widely in how qualified they are to speak on their subject, and have sometimes been manipulated into speaking on an unexpected question or are confronted with some accusation just to get an emotional response. TV news stations manufacture drama to get more viewers as well as clicks and shares on the clip that will later be put on the web. That is not what news should look like. There is no substance to be found in it.

Gossip and Accusations as News

It has become common to report the fact that someone said something as if that is news in itself. These kinds of reports usually consist of an accusation, the other person's denial, and no determination about whether there is any truth to the accusation or not. Similarly, a news organization may report simply that some prominent person speculated that something "might" be true.

Anyone can say anything—that doesn't mean there's a shred of truth to what they say, or that there's any point in anyone paying attention to it.

No accusation should ever be reported until journalists have verified evidence to support that there's truth in the substance of the accusation, not just that the accusation was made. It is not news to say that people gossip and make up nasty things about each other—or that they sometimes manipulate the media "narrative" by saying things they know aren't true.

Paying attention to such irresponsible gossip demeans us all.

News Blogs

Today many of us read about the news on blogs. Some blogs are written by experienced and ethical journalists who are using this new format to reach a wider audience. That's a great thing. However, literally anyone can write whatever they want on a blog. They can invent stories completely, they can fake their credentials, and they can use a lot of links to present an appearance of basing their writing on connections to what others are saying, even if those links are actually to sites that say unrelated or contradictory things, or are other fake articles.

Any blog should have an "about" section saying who the writer is. Some blog writers do not reveal their real names for privacy reasons but explain that they have a relevant professional affiliation. In those cases you can only judge their reliability on the content of what they write. Follow the golden rule: look for the evidence. Do they explain their evidence and reasoning to support their claims? Follow all the links—do the linked sites say what the author suggests they will say? Does the evidence presented come from legitimate sources like independent statistics bureaus?

For blogs written by authors who are open about their identity, a quick independent search can usually confirm the credentials they provide for themselves, and give you more information about institutions they are affiliated with. See Chapter 3 for more information about how to weigh this kind of evidence.

Many—if not most—blogs presenting opinions on political and cultural affairs are basically the same as listening to a random stranger in a coffee shop, and you should treat it that way. You may learn something interesting, but you have no way of knowing if there's any truth to it without doing some further investigating.

Professional Fact-Checkers

None of us has the time to zealously verify every piece of news we see. But it is worth our time to verify our most common sources of news before continuing to rely on them, and to check particularly shocking or disturbing news items or articles that motivate us to act in some way.

At other times, a shortcut is to rely on those sites that specialize in assessing the truth of political news claims like Politifact.org and Factcheck.org, the fact-checking service at the Washington Post, or OpenSecrets.org, which tracks the influence of money in politics. Still more resources can be found by consulting the International Fact-Checking Network hosted by the Poynter Institute (Poynter.org), a non-profit dedicated to supporting quality journalism, or by consulting the Duke Reporter's Lab (ReportersLab.org), which maintains a list of fact-checking sites around the world.

The most important thing to remember in using such sites is to read not just their final assessment of a claim, but their analysis of how they determined that verdict. The analysis should show you their evidence and reasoning, so you can judge it for yourself. They are also a good model of how to verify such stories on your own. Not every analysis on such sites is perfect or complete, but they can be a useful and time-saving tool when used mindfully.

Chapter Three

Dealing with People

We are surrounded by people who claim to have some authority over information. And there are times when, even if we had the best skills in the world, we simply lack the time or access to do all the research ourselves. We are then forced to trust others who say they know what we don't. How can we find people worth trusting? What does it mean to be an "expert"?

There are a lot of bad sources out there. There are people who fake credentials, who are lying in order to sell you something or to get your support for their cause, and people who just don't know what they're talking about, whether or not they have the best intentions. The people presented on television as "experts" may have been chosen for how well they look and speak on TV more than for their actual expertise. People who have power or wealth are often falsely assumed to be experts because we admire or envy them.

Since evidence and reasoning are all that really matter, the most important thing you can do to protect yourself from fraudsters and to maintain skepticism of even well-meaning authorities is to look for the evidence and reasoning, and if you don't see any, don't trust it. When you do see it, test it—and if it doesn't pass the test, don't trust it.

We must test our sources, because it is equally costly either to reject any outside authority or to accept only those sources that reinforce the beliefs we already have. Both actions close us off from new information we might need.

Who Can We Believe?

There are several rules of thumb that can work as shortcuts to identify sources that are more likely to be reliable than others, though none are fool-proof. Sources that are subject to some form of accountability are always preferable to sources with none, but we must approach either with a critical eye for evidence and reasoning.

Remember also that there is a broad range of how you respond to a source between "fully accept" and "fully reject." You can read with skepticism and an open mind, you can file away what you read without coming to a judgment on it, and you can accept some parts while dismissing others (assuming you base those decisions on reasoning and evidence, not what fits whatever prior beliefs you brought to the text).

Sources That Are Already Vetted

Web addresses that end in ".org," ".edu," or ".gov" are at least not selling something. Websites on ".edu" servers are hosted by an educational institution and should contain content that was created for educational purposes by qualified educators. Websites ending in ".gov" are official sites of local, state, or federal government and are accountable to government oversight.

Academic publishers put all their publications through a process of peer review to vet its reliability. Some of this material is available for free online (this is called "open-access" publishing—see Chapters 8 and 9 for specific examples). Much more is available either through online journal databases that charge a fee (often exorbitant for individuals, but free at point of use for those with an affiliation at a subscribing academic institution), or through books sold by online retailers in the usual way. Publishers with the words "university press" in their name always use peer review, but so do some others such as Routledge, Palgrave, Ashgate, Berghahn, Brill, Wiley-Blackwell, Verso, Roman & Littlefield, or New Academia Press. A publisher's website will disclose whether all or part of their book catalogs are peer-reviewed, though that information may be tucked away under "submission guidelines" or "author information."

Some institutes, think tanks, and journalistic outlets are open about how they vet and fact-check the data or analysis they produce. If an organization is not being transparent about this process, that in itself is a bad sign. These kinds of organizations range from completely partisan propaganda machines to independent public resources, so tread carefully.

Many professions have organizations that are meant to oversee ethical standards. The lawyers' bar association is the best known, but journalists and academics also have professional organizations. They are not all equally strict or effective in imposing standards on practitioners, but looking up the relevant professional organization for a particular kind of source can tell you what the expected standards are and whether or in what way practitioners can be held accountable.

It is often possible to look up an individual's educational and professional experience or credentials online. If they do not have an official bio on a website associated with where they work, this information might be on LinkedIn.com or another professional social network, such as Academia.edu. Credentials may mean a lot, or nothing much, so they should be assessed in context. Is the person's degree in a field relevant to what you find them talking about? Is it from an accredited institution with a strong reputation in that field? How advanced is their degree relative to the level of expertise they claim? Is their professional experience in an appropriately related field? What is their job title, and what responsibilities does that imply? How many years of relevant experience do they have? If you're not sure, search company or institutional names, job titles, and degree fields and levels to clarify the person's background.

While looking at the background of a source, also ask whether they have access to the information needed to draw their conclusions. Researchers need access to data, experimental tools, documentation, or participants in an inquiry. Journalists, pundits, whistleblowers, government officials and others rely on being able to witness events or speak first-hand with the people or documents involved. If the sources of information are in another language, the expert needs to speak that language fluently or rely on the trustworthiness of someone who does. If the information requires analysis, the expert needs the resources and time to carry it out.

Warning Signs of Unreliable Sources

There are also signs we can look for that suggest things are not as they should be. Red flags that suggest a source is not reliable include:

- Information presented alongside efforts to sell products or services (this is not always a problem, of course, but it is a sign telling us to look further and maintain skepticism).

- Information presented with no explanation of where it came from, or phrases like "people say" or "I heard" or "this is going around." Gossip is the most unreliable kind of information short of deliberate lying, and it should be dismissed out of hand. Only independent confirmation from named sources with some authority to know the truth can be taken seriously.

- A source that is not transparent about its goals or point of view. There is nothing inherently unreliable about a source that is "slanted" toward a particular "side" (see below), as long as it is open about its position and what the position is based on. Most websites, whether they belong to a large organization or one blogger, have some kind of "about" section or "mission statement" that explain its purposes and point of view. If this is absent or deliberately vague, the site needs further scrutiny.

- Any information that appeals to the reader's emotional reactions rather than reasoning may be trying to manipulate us. Look for dire predictions phrased in colorful language, especially language that addresses you directly, like "The detergent you're using will destroy your washing machine!" or "What you don't know about your water will poison your children!"

- Information presented by someone with a financial or other personal stake in how it is used. Professional researchers are generally paid to produce research regardless of the result, which should, along with professional ethics, encourage objectivity. But there are for-profit research bodies that are sometimes hard to distinguish from independent ones, and politically slanted organizations. Look for disclosures about funding.

- Information presented by someone with power or wealth that assumes you will trust it because of the position of this person, without evidence or reasoning to support the claims. We tend to trust people we see as "successful," on the assumption that they got where they are by being better than the rest of us. This is a faulty assumption. While some people inherit power or wealth, fall into it by accident, or seize it through illegitimate paths, even those who have thoroughly earned their success are not experts at everything just because they succeeded in one area.

What a Real Expert Looks Like

A real expert cares more about truth—that is, the evidence and logical reasoning that demonstrate reliable facts—than allegiance to any "side" or investment in a particular course of action. Real experts qualify their claims and admit freely to what they don't know as well as sharing the evidence and reasoning that their knowledge is based on. Experts are people who know how things work in their field. They know the steps to take to get things done, they know what the potential obstacles are, and ways to try to get around them. We should look for evidence of these kinds of knowledge and disclosures about methods to decide whether a source is worth listening to. We should remember that real expertise is much harder and slower and more expensive to achieve than faking it.

Everything You Know about Academia Is Wrong

A common myth about the most obvious category of experts, professional scholars, is that their knowledge is esoteric and useless in "real" life. This myth is based partly on cultural memory of what American higher education was like during a brief heyday following World War II when college enrollments skyrocketed because of the GI Bill and faculty enjoyed a pretty sweet gig. Most film and TV depictions are based on stereotypes of this period, with pipe-wielding professors in tweeds pontificating about poetry to adoring students.

Other myths stem from the 1960s and 70s when many scholarly disciplines were reassessed to take in new "postmodern" theories about cultural relativity and the deconstruction of what seems to be real. Much of this sounds like nonsense to most people. The version most people hear is nonsense. The popular versions of these ideas are usually misunderstood or sometimes satirical takes on the originals. To get the real versions, you pretty much have to take a university class—it takes a lot of context to explain.

Today's reality is that with declining funding the number of full-time faculty positions has dramatically dropped, so that every accredited institution in the country can boast the best-trained and most productive scholars. Competition for jobs has also pushed scholars to better articulate the connections between their work and the public interest (the connection was always there, but it was not always easy to find or well explained). Doctoral education and university teaching are defined by critical thinking: it is the basis of all scholarship and it is what professors do all day. We practice and teach critical thinking.

Most people are at least aware of how "STEM" fields (science, technology, engineering and math) are useful in everyday life. We are much less aware of the role of social scientists and humanities scholars as specialists in information analysis, even though their work is equally important and useful, not least because information is the defining resource of our age. Scholars of information distinguish between fact and fantasy, develop and teach methods of making sense of information in all its forms, and help us all to find meaning in the chaos of life. Today's professors as a group are more diverse, far more accomplished, and far less well paid than ever before. And without the information they collectively sort, vet, teach, and produce, we will be lost.

Other Kinds of Experts

Scholars are by no means the only kind of recognized expert, however. Expertise usually takes one of the following forms, and can involve people from all walks of life and all fields of knowledge. What makes them expert is having mastery of a subject or skill (which does not imply any special knowledge or skill in other fields, though it may offer some perspective on closely related areas).

Expert observers – Expert witnesses in a trial are a form of observer expert, but other kinds of observers range from natural scientists whose research is based on observation and measurement to professionals in education, medicine, law, or finance who have accumulated broad experience of how their fields work and can explain these phenomena to others, to other forms of consultants, from home appraisers to security specialists, as well as people who can discern differences undetectable to others, like food tasters and those who detect forgeries in art or currency.

Expert analysts – Analysts and diagnosticians are people who can identify patterns in information and their significance, from car mechanics to ultrasound readers to psychologists to literary critics to statisticians.

Expert practitioners – People who have practiced a set of skills to the point of being able to perform them at a highly successful level on demand are expert practitioners, no matter what it is they do, including architects, artists, athletes, engineers, writers, salespeople, managers, surgeons, cooks, pilots, craftspeople, and many others.

Some forms of expertise combine these categories, of course. Scientists observe and analyze, and many must have various practical skills in order to carry out their research—to take just one example of a profession that combines all three forms of expertise. But it is worth thinking about expertise in its different aspects because many of us unconsciously view "real" expertise as involving only one of these types. We tend to privilege one over the others based on our own experiences, but that is a limited view.

Why We Don't Like to Listen to Experts

One of the difficulties our brains present us when we hear surprising things from an expert is that this challenge to our own experience or expectations makes us want to dig in to defend ourselves rather than hearing and objectively weighing the new information. One way to counteract this tendency is to frequently and honestly assess the limits of our own knowledge.

A Little Knowledge Is a Dangerous Thing

Every one of us is expert in some fields of knowledge, totally ignorant of others, and partially aware of still other areas. But we can often know a great deal about one aspect of a question and mistake that partial knowledge for mastery of the whole field. For example, since nearly everyone has been a student for many years, most people think they know and understand what education is all about. However, this is as inaccurate as believing we can perform a root canal because we have faithfully visited a dentist as a patient every six months.

All Knowledge Is Good, and Useful

Though we tend to privilege the kind of knowledge we rely on most in our own lives, in reality each form of knowledge is no better or worse than others. Each is simply better suited to particular kinds of questions. It would be silly to imagine you could learn to fly a plane from reading books alone, and it is equally silly to imagine you can understand the economics of nations because you have run a successful business. Mastering the theory of child development may be a helpful aid in parenting, but does not in itself make you a capable parent. Being a master handspinner does not mean you understand the impact of the spinning jenny on the industrial revolution and modern history, any more than being an expert on the history of pre-industrial Europe will help you make a sweater out of a pile of sheep's wool and a few sticks.

All knowledge and skills deserve respect. Advanced or expert knowledge has special value no matter what field it's in, but it is of course never perfect. And even the best expert knowledge in one field has limited reach into adjacent fields and none at all into unrelated fields. Practical knowledge is not better than theoretical and vice versa: they simply have different uses in different contexts.

When you need to saw a board in half, don't pick up a hammer.

Keeping Perspective

As an exercise, make a detailed list of the things you know best and how you know them. Add a second list of related fields that your expertise may give you some insight on. Now make a third list of fields unrelated to your personal knowledge. That list could be infinite, but for the purpose of the exercise, make it at least as long as your other lists, and as varied as possible.

Keep these lists in mind as you encounter other people's claims to expertise in various realms. In some areas your knowledge will allow you to vet the information you encounter, to ask productive questions about it, or to recognize that you need to seek reliable guides to help you navigate uncharted waters.

Is This Person for Real?

Of course, sometimes a person on the internet just isn't who they say they are. Here are a few quick ways to vet a person's identity online:

- Do a separate search to confirm anything they say about their background or credentials. Not all details can be confirmed through publicly available websites, but direct contradictions are a strong warning sign, and a total absence of confirmation is a weaker but still real warning.

- If you are contacted by someone who claims to represent a company, independently look up contact information for that company and ask them through those channels whether the communication was legitimate. It is a classic "phishing" scam to contact people as if from a bank or utility company and demand payment or personal information (see Chapter 7).

- The major social media sites like Facebook and Twitter verify the identity of celebrities and other public figures, marking verified accounts with a notched blue circle containing a check mark next to the username. Don't believe an account belongs to a public figure without this mark (and check that the mark is not Photoshopped onto a profile picture, which anyone can do—it should be a separate image placed in a position that users can't edit).

- Social networks, online forums, and review sites often feature so-called "sock puppets," or multiple accounts created by one person in order to leave an impression of many people all agreeing with an idea or approving a product. Check the profile of any suspicious user to see if they've been active on the site long and have posted on other topics. Also examine the kinds of words and the style of writing of the accounts that seem to all agree, for signs that they may all have been written by one person.

- "Troll" is internet slang for someone who takes part in an online conversation only to create trouble or get strong reactions out of people. Classic signs of "troll" behavior are people who never directly respond to questions asked of them, who post repetitively or escalate dramatic language or provocative statements, and who engage regularly in "straw man" and "red herring" fallacies (that is, they bring up extreme scenarios that no one was really discussing, or raise issues out of left field to derail the conversation). The only thing to do with a troll is to stop "feeding" them. Ignore them by using whatever settings are available to block or hide that thread, forum, page, or user from your view. Continue engaging productively with other users who are also ignoring the troll.

Engaging with People Who Disagree

The internet is famous for terrible comment sections and wild-west style forums where "flame wars" dominate over civil discussion. There are trolls and sock puppets and other nefarious personages online who make it more difficult to have real conversations. Many websites are now learning how to filter out the trolls, though, and many people really do value and want to take part in civil discussion.

The biggest problem today is that real interpersonal engagement online requires more than a civil tone, kindness, or good intentions. Engaging with people who disagree with you requires that you truly consider their views by entertaining the possibility that they may be right and you may be wrong. Of course, you may conclude at the end of that process that you still disagree, and that's fine. But until you actually make the effort to fully understand and try out the other person's position, your disagreement is baseless.

Exercises for Engaging

Considering a contrary point of view with full seriousness and a genuinely open mind is extraordinarily difficult. It requires that we do the mental gymnastics of temporarily suspending our own views and experience while we imaginatively put ourselves in someone else's shoes. Try the following exercises to aid this process:

1. Ask questions, lots of questions, without asserting your own views. Really listen to the answers. Many of us assume we already know where someone else is coming from, especially if we have already lumped them into a category or type. You have to let this go and allow the person speak for themselves. When you don't fully understand, ask more questions until you do.

2. If what you're hearing sounds totally stupid to you, remember that very often other people's views sound that way to us because we're the ones missing key information, which the speaker is taking for granted or hasn't had a chance to mention yet. Ask more questions to find out.

3. Pay close attention to the words the other person uses, and believe what they say, and only what they say, without adding assumptions based on who you think they are. If they are

inconsistent in what they say, ask more questions to tease out what they really mean.

4. You can respect personal experiences and individual expertise, while still recognizing reliable information about the larger picture. Be careful not to confuse "anecdata"—anecdotal evidence, or personal stories—with actual statistics, and encourage the other person to be equally clear about the difference. Both forms of evidence have value (assuming the personal stories are first-hand), but they are not equally illuminating on all kinds of questions (see Chapter 6).

5. No communication can happen without mutually recognizing the dictionary definitions of words and established rules of logic. If the person you're speaking with refuses to do this, the conversation cannot continue. At the same time, though, some complex ideas cannot be conveyed with simple dictionary definitions. Everyone should define any words they are using in a specialized way, and justify their need to rely on special words by explaining why simpler words cannot convey the intended meaning or are so awkward they hold back the conversation. Every definition will include exceptions, but this does not negate the definition. If there are more exceptions than otherwise, though, formulate a new, more accurate definition.

6. When you make your own claims, qualify them appropriately and avoid exaggeration. Say only what you can back up with evidence and reasoning.

7. Explain the basis of your claims. If they're based on personal experience, say so. If they are based on external evidence and reasoning, explain it.

8. Don't pretend to things you don't believe just to be polite and get along. This reinforces divisions in the long run. If you're going to play devil's advocate, though, admit that that's what you're doing.

9. Avoid emotional language, and responding to emotional appeals. Address ideas, but not the person behind them, and hold the other person to doing the same.

10. Slow down. Although the internet makes it possible to communicate in real time without regard to distance, we are

not required to respond immediately to anything. Try typing up what you want to say, then walking away and doing something else before sending or posting it. Read it again after your break and consider whether you can rephrase your point in a more productive way.

11. Whenever you're addressing another person on the internet, remember the human being behind the bits and bytes. Picture the person as specifically as possible. Add details like an outfit, a hairstyle, a chair, a background, and maybe a pet to humanize them in your imagination.

12. Wait—who did you just picture? Did you picture a specific person you know who this internet person reminds you of, or a stereotype of someone you think the person on the other side of the screen might fit? That's not going to work. Deliberately choose visual details that are random and mis-matched. This allows you to see the person who really is out there as fully human: a unique individual made of flesh and blood.

13. It is famously hard to read tone on the internet, but what you can do is just always read what other people have written in a pleasant, earnest, and open-minded tone. That may not be the way they actually wrote it, but if you assume it is, you'll have a pleasanter experience and be more likely to nudge the conversation into a more productive direction. Maintaining this stance is of course incredibly difficult, so give yourself a break, but try to do it when you can.

14. Assume that any person who is bothering you on the internet is having a really, really bad day. Because every day, many people really are having a terrible time and deserve a little extra patience. Whether or not that's really true of the person you might be dealing with, assuming so is a kindness that makes life easier for everyone.

15. Do your best to maintain a sense of humor. Some conversations are about such serious topics that jokes or silly examples can themselves be insulting, but in most cases inserting lightness into a conversation can help all parties stay on an even emotional keel, and therefore reason more effectively.

Reading Perspectives

The internet is full of individual perspectives. These range from the posts of ordinary people on Facebook or other forums to blogs to "think pieces" by established journalists and editorials from recognized news organizations. But the fact that information now reaches us in much the same way from many different sources—all as words on a screen, regardless of origin, source, or context—has made it more difficult to distinguish opinion from claim, fact from story, and prejudice from point of view.

This Is So Ugly

Many people are tempted to dismiss anything personal as "just biased." Others get offended when a personal reflection on a subject fails to account for the reader's own experience. On other occasions we confuse cause and effect by assuming that one person's experience of how an event or phenomenon has affected people is also an explanation of why it happened. All of these natural and normal reactions to the storm of decentralized information on the internet are contributing to making many of us feel more angry, divided, and close-minded. For that reason, it's worth putting effort into finding better ways to navigate this minefield of conflicting personal perspectives.

Not Everyone Is Biased All the Time

The first point to recognize is the difference between bias and point of view. We all understand bias to be a bad thing, and the accusation of being biased is flung around often. Bias is a systematic prejudice. It is a belief that is maintained despite exposure to contrary evidence. Usually such prejudices are maintained because the believer gains something from them, whether that's psychological comfort, material benefit, or something else.

A point of view, on the other hand, simply describes how any one individual person sees the world. This view is naturally limited— no one can know or see everything at once—but it is a view shaped by evidence.

For example, I am biased in believing my children are the cutest children that have ever lived, because I continue to believe they are the cutest no matter how many other children I see. This belief makes me feel rather good about myself, since I produced these children.

But my conclusion that I can fit more glasses into my dishwasher by putting them between the vertical spokes rather than on them is based on the evidence of having tried it both ways. This conclusion is of course limited to my experience with my own dishwasher, and the sizes of glassware I own. The evidence of a different dishwasher or different glasses may legitimately lead to a different conclusion. But my conclusion based on my dishwasher is not biased as long as I can acknowledge those limits on my experience.

In a similar way, when we read people's personal experiences online, we must look for the evidence behind their claims before we dismiss their testimony as "biased," especially if it contradicts our own experience. We must also look for the limits of that person's knowledge and experience, as well as our own, to reconcile how we can come to different reasoned conclusions based on different evidence.

Just because someone has a stated position doesn't mean they are biased, just that they are not neutral. Neutrality is not a virtue, it's just a state of not knowing or deciding. People who know—who have assessed relevant evidence and come to a conclusion—should have formed a position. Such a position is always worth taking seriously, even if we eventually conclude otherwise for ourselves, based on other evidence and reasoning. What we cannot do is dismiss such a position as biased. When we are tempted to do so, we should ask ourselves what personal needs of our own are driving that temptation.

Insults versus Criticism

The difference between an insult and a criticism is the difference between a pointless fight and a productive discussion. Insults attack a person's characteristics rather than their ideas or actions, such as the statement, "you're stupid." Insults and slurs serve no productive purpose. They're just mean.

Criticisms identify real flaws in words or actions (attacking what people say or do, not who they are). Such flaws can be explained, with evidence or reasoning, as the cause of some real problem or harm.

Criticisms can be stated in a gentle way or in a harsh way. They are more effective when they are not harshly stated, but the tone of the statement doesn't affect whether the criticism is accurate or not. No one wants to be told, "you're ignorant," but we are all actually ignorant of many things. It simply means there's something we don't know. However, it would be more productive to say, "did you know about ____?"

In some cases, though, there may not be a nice way to phrase a valid and necessary criticism. And even the best phrasing isn't likely to remove the sting: no one enjoys being criticized, even in a nice tone. Even when criticisms hurt though, they are evidence-based statements that should be evaluated like any other, not returned back on the speaker with the equivalent of the schoolyard taunt, "I know you are but what am I?"

If a criticism is unfounded, attack the evidence and reasoning that should support it, not the person who made it, even if they used harsher words than were necessary.

Proportion and Values

Each of us prioritizes some concerns over others, and as a result one of the ways we can come into conflict even when we mostly share essential values is when we disagree over proportion.

If two people agree, for example, that a ban on large-sized sodas is a bad idea and that a ban on immigration is a bad idea, one person might see the two propositions as two examples of the same rule. That person opposes government bans on principle, and puts a higher priority on individual choice than most other things. Another person might also oppose both bans, but see the ban on immigration as a completely different and much worse problem than banning large soda portions, because it restricts and possibly punishes a certain group of people in life-changing ways, while the soda ban might be seen as a minor encroachment on individuals' luxury choices.

We are sometimes too broad when we talk to each other in terms of "agreement" or "disagreement." We can talk more productively if we speak more clearly about what we value, how we prioritize those values, and think through whether we are responding to what we hear in proportion to its importance, both in the sense of how serious a problem might be based on external evidence, and in the sense of its importance according to our own personal values.

Try changing the words you use in discussions about contentious issues to avoid final takeaways or bottom lines and instead emphasize assumptions, tendencies, values, suspicions, questions, and relative importance.

No One Lives in Order to Hurt You

No one has ever experienced anything in order to make you feel bad. They are just living their life, as you are living yours. When someone shares their personal experience, you should assume they are speaking to you, not at you. They are trying to communicate what they experienced, not trying to edit or judge what you experienced, since they don't know what you experienced. Remembering this fact can keep most of us from taking offense most of the time.

About Representation

No one perspective can, by definition, represent everyone else (it shouldn't try, because that would be stereotyping). A perspective is personal, reflecting only on the person behind it. We do not need to demand diversity from within each perspective presented to the world. Diversity comes from variety within a group of perspectives. (This logical error is at the base of most internet wars over television shows.)

The Trouble with Groups

One of the most difficult problems we face in relating to each other on the virtual plane is to navigate the differences between individual and group experiences and beliefs. A common point of contention you see in internet debates is about whether some member of a group is representative of the whole group. This is a pointless debate, and we'd all be better off if we could check ourselves against the following simple rules about social groups.

- Every group is diverse. Never assume that being a member of a certain group means that any individual in it shares all views with the other members, has the same reasons for being a member, or thinks or acts in concert with the rest of the group. A Pokemon Go club, for example, would likely include people of different levels of skill and commitment, and probably a few people with little interest who are just there to support a friend or to meet people.

- At the same time, someone who joins a group is endorsing it, at least up to whatever point that person explicitly states—and acts on—their objections to some part of the group's stated purposes. If you join a Facebook group intended to lobby your town council for new sidewalks, people are going to rightly assume you want new sidewalks, unless you actually say "I joined that on a friend's recommendation, and have now changed my mind," and then proceed to leave the group.

- The best definition of any group is one settled on by multiple independent observers as an accurate description of the group's intentional actions, without judgment—if such a definition exists. The second-best definition of any group is how it defines itself. Beware of definitions articulated only by a group's opponents. For example, scholars of the Soviet Union refer to the political system from about 1922 to 1953 as "Stalinism" rather than "Communism" or "Totalitarianism" because that word more precisely describes what was unique to that period and what was linked to the person of Stalin, while still taking into account the USSR's officially Marxist ideology and Stalin's authoritarianism. While the USSR referred to itself as a "Communist" regime, technically Communism (as the ultimate achievement of socialist transformation) was their ambition, not a reality they claimed to have reached. "Totalitarianism" is a term used by Western observers to conflate the Soviet Union with their most recently defeated enemy, fascism. While both fascist and Communist regimes were authoritarian, violent, and expressed expansionist ambitions, the term is not very accurate because it ignores their many differences and the fact that neither regime really achieved "total" control.

- Beware of groups that deliberately define themselves in misleading ways to obscure their purpose. Judge people by their actions more than their words. For example, the Nazi Party is short for the "National Socialist Party" even though it was violently opposed to socialism. Socialism proper is an internationalist movement, so "national" socialism was meant to redirect the mass appeal of socialism in a new, nationalistic direction (defined in practice by notions of racial superiority and a massively powerful, intrusive government, and having nothing to do with economic equality).

- All movements or social groups change over time and have divisions within them. If you want to understand a group, understand its divisions and evolutions. Acknowledge the existence of these divisions and evolutions when you talk about or judge the group. Feminism, for example, is a political movement that has developed over more than a century in many countries around the world. There are socialist feminists, nationalist feminists, feminists who embrace "militant" tactics and feminists who renounce them. There have been feminists who focused almost solely on the right to vote, and feminists who believed the right to vote was a minor issue. Feminism has sometimes been dominated by middle-class white women and their issues, while other feminists have focused their efforts on working-class and minority women.

- Groups can't be held accountable for every action of each member, but should be held accountable for actions endorsed by the group as part of its group identity. Understanding the defining purposes of the group and how this is reflected in the actions of leaders or majorities is essential to judging whether the group itself is responsible for the individual actions of members. For example, a club called "Operation Chaos" that forms with the purpose of randomly shifting books around on library shelves should be held accountable for the mess they make. But a research club that meets in the library to study shouldn't be held collectively responsible when a member fails to put a book she used back in the proper place.

- When talking about groups, we can all benefit from being as specific as possible. Instead of referring to "people who hate sports," much less a pejorative term like "nerds," we can say "most people I've met who don't enjoy football on TV."

- When someone else refers to a group with qualifiers like "most" or "usually," you must acknowledge that they have already accounted for exceptions, and there is no need to point out that "not everyone in the group is like that." Those kinds of comments derail discussions and justifiably annoy people.

- When someone else does generalize about a group—specifically stating that members of some group, as a whole, do or do not share some characteristic or perform some action—you are in turn justified in pointing out their error.

- The existence of small numbers of exceptions does not nullify the group characteristics. Thus, it is true that network news is watched more by older people, even if you are a young person who loves CBS news. This is the difference between anecdata and real data.

A more productive way to discuss the responsibility of individuals versus groups is to discuss the specifics of evidence telling us who is involved, how many of those people are or are not demonstrably associated with certain ideas or actions, and so on.

Chapter Four

Reading Arguments

When you read an article online that tries to persuade you of something, you're reading an argument. When your Facebook friend makes a claim about why or how something happens, that's an argument, too. When an expert explains why or how something happens or recommends a future action, that too is an argument.

What Is an Argument?

An argument, in this sense, is a series of claims supported by evidence and reasoning (that is, we're not talking about fights, name-calling, or flame wars). The first, most important way to understand and evaluate the validity of an argument is to recognize these parts.

- *Claims* are arguable statements. Any statement that reasonable people can disagree about, such as, "Macs are better than PCs," is a claim.

- *Evidence* consists of real-world facts or data. For example, it is a fact that Apple is more proprietorial about software than other computer companies.

- *Reasoning* is the logic that links evidence to claims. For example: "because Mac software is so tightly controlled, it's more reliable and easier to use." That statement explains why someone could reach the given claim based on the available evidence.

An effective argument should be open about its claims, evidence, and reasoning, which allows you to judge for yourself whether you accept all or any of it.

Fake Arguments

Someone who tries to convince you of something without explaining their evidence and reasoning is asking you to simply trust them. Trust needs to be earned, though. A track record of deserving trust is encouraging and in some cases may be all we have to go on, but ideally we should at least have evidence that the person has appropriate knowledge or skills to lead them to a reliable conclusion.

One way that people can try to deceive us is to construct what sounds like a logical argument by using words like "evidence" and having an organized structure, making references to outside sources, and using connecting words like "however," or "thus" that create an effect that the writer is following the rules of logic. But the content needs to match the form.

More about Evidence

Evidence is information that exists out in the world, independently of whether a claim is true or not. To defend a claim, we point to these facts about the world and explain how they are a reflection of the truth of our claims. (That explanation is the "reasoning" part.) Most people understand "evidence" to mean data and statistics, and these are explored in detail in Chapter 6.

Observations

But evidence can also be an observation, like "the sky is blue." Of course, one person's observation that the sky is blue at one particular moment does not mean the sky isn't overcast where another person is observing it, or dark when both people look at it later that night.

The most important thing to know about personal observations as evidence is their limits: one person can observe that "all the babies I know are walking before they're a year old," and that can be perfectly true, but it does not actually tell us anything about the age at which most babies walk (later than 12 months), since that one person is not observing a representative sample of all babies.

We also have to ask, if we want to take someone's personal observation as evidence, whether that person does have first-hand access to what they say they observed, and what are the chances that they might lie about their experience? Do they have any motivation to lie? Any history of dishonesty?

Documentation

The simplest form of textual evidence is documentation. A paper record (or today, a secure digital record kept on an independent server) documents that something happened at a certain date, time, or place. Your birth certificate is documentation of when and where you were born, and who was recorded at that time as your mother and father. Receipts are documentation of a purchase, and boarding passes are documentation of travel.

Another form of documentation is when someone claims that a certain person supports some idea or action, and a document or video (video is a "text" in a loose sense of the term) shows the person saying something positive about that idea or action.

Documentation is pretty irrefutable, assuming we check that nothing about the document, audio, or video were altered.

Texts as Fallacy

But there's another common way people use statements as evidence that is actually a fallacy. This is when we quote some authority agreeing with us as "evidence" to support our own claims. We are saying, "look, this other, important person agrees with me!" This is known as the "appeal to authority fallacy." The closely related "bandwagon fallacy" is when we use the fact that our view is shared by a lot of other people as "evidence."

The problem with this reasoning is that anyone can be misguided or mistaken. It doesn't matter who, or how many people, agree with us because they could all be equally wrong for all we know, without evidence to judge them on. If an expert on the subject agrees with the point you want to make, share the evidence and reasoning that the expert's opinion is based on. That's the part that's convincing (or not), on its own merits—not the name, status, or number of people who said it.

Textual Interpretation

A third way to use text or statements as evidence can be useful, but is complicated. This is textual interpretation. To interpret a text is to read the context and subtext of a statement to infer what the speaker may have meant (including possibly unconscious intentions) and what the statement might imply or lead to regardless of how the speaker intended it. Such interpretations can never, of course, be definitive. But they are also not arbitrary when they are done properly.

For example, in both the book and film of Harry Potter and the Order of the Phoenix, the fictional Hogwarts School of Witchcraft and Wizardry gets a new headmistress named Professor Umbridge, who imposes a series of new rules, including a rule that students may not gather in groups. The text of that rule—the letter of the law—is straightforward in the sense that we understand it easily, but not straightforward in that Umbridge's reasons for the rule—what exactly she was afraid of if students met in groups—are not stated. The context is that Professor Umbridge was appointed by the Ministry of Magic to replace the previous headmaster, Dumbledore, who had tried to warn the wizarding world that the evil Lord Voldemort had come back to his full powers to threaten wizardingkind, but the Ministry didn't believe him. In the story, the student Hermione listens to Umbridge's speech to the school and concludes that the Ministry is trying to interfere at Hogwarts in order to prevent students from supporting Dumbledore's efforts to prepare for Voldemort's attacks, and the decree against student groups seems to fit into this neatly. It suggests that the decree against groups is specifically intended to stop groups from supporting Dumbledore. What Hermione figures out between the lines of Umbridge's literal statements is called subtext.

Another familiar example of the relationship between text, context, and subtext is when a teenager writes a note about nothing important to another teenager. The context in this example is that the first teenager has a crush on the second teenager. The subtext is what's going on between the lines of the note, which is to say, there's much more there than what is written in plain English. The writer of the note is trying to show their own interest and gauge whether the recipient is also interested. The recipient of the note may or may not understand this subtext, but it is there either way. Almost everyone has some experience of that kind of subtext, and knows that it is as real as it is unstated.

The interpretation of texts is about how both context and subtext can enrich our understanding of any text. Such interpretations are not arbitrary because they are based on the specific wording of the text and concrete circumstances surrounding how the text was made, presented, and received by an audience. But the interpretation is also not definitive, because we cannot fully know people's intentions—even if they do state what they think or what they want to present as their intentions.

Textual evidence must be understood as tentative, but it should also be taken seriously so far as it is grounded in the real details and subtle distinctions of meaning inherent in any text or speech, written or recorded.

How to Test Claims

Before we can agree or disagree with a claim, we need to not only question the evidence and reasoning given, but also consider what other evidence or reasoning might be relevant but wasn't included.

- Ask what other conclusions could be drawn from the same evidence
- Look independently for sources that provide reliable and relevant evidence that was not used
- Ask what else the given evidence might suggest
- Question the reasoning by looking for unexplained leaps and logical fallacies
- Ask whether a different line of reasoning could lead to different conclusions

Noticing Flaws in Reasoning

It's not important to know the names of logical fallacies in order to judge whether someone's reasoning is sound. Probably the most common logical flaw is simply what we call a "leap," when someone doesn't fully explain, and may not have fully thought through, all the implications of their claim, evidence, and reasoning.

For example, in response to hearing that some people get dangerous ideas on the internet, a person might claim that the only solution is to ban the internet. This claim leaps past the fact that the vast majority of what happens on the internet is not dangerous, the difficulty of actually banning the entire internet, and the many alternative ways that the problem of "dangerous ideas" could be addressed.

In addition, the following logical fallacies are other common ways that reasoning can break down or fail to make the intended point.

- Cherry-picking – choosing evidence that supports your claims, while ignoring evidence that contradicts it

- Straw man – raising extreme scenarios that aren't really relevant to the discussion

- Red herring – distracting attention from the key points by changing the subject (so-called "tone policing" is related: when you distract from the substance of a discussion by criticizing the tone in which people talk about it)

- Circular reasoning – using elements of your claim as evidence that the claim is true, or trying to support your claim by restating it in different words ("You have to go to bed because it's bedtime.")

- Slippery slope – assuming that one action must automatically lead to other, more extreme ones

- Black and white thinking – assuming that there are only two possibilities and that the two are completely separate

- Look who's talking – saying that because someone has done one thing wrong, they can't judge wrongs done by others

- Hasty generalization – when you leap from one or a few examples to assume things about a whole group ("One teenager I know loves to knit hats. All teenagers must love to knit hats.")

- I'm entitled to my opinion – when you invoke your "right" to think whatever you want as a defense of your position. It's an absence of defense for the position.

Qualified Claims

Some claims may have valid evidence and reasoning that does not depend on fallacies, but still not hold in all circumstances. In the example about Macs versus PCs described above, it would be a valid critique of that reasoning to say that some people prefer greater flexibility and access, and so for them Macs are not, in fact, better. You could equally argue that ease of use versus flexibility are not the most important factors to base the comparison on.

The strongest kinds of claims are qualified to account for the limits of their evidence or reasoning. Thus, "Macs are better than PCs for many novice computer users, or anyone else who prioritizes ease of use over flexibility" is a much stronger and more defensible claim than "Macs are better than PCs." But note that it is still arguable. If a statement is inarguably true, then it is a fact, not a claim.

Claims That Don't Apply to You Still Aren't Wrong

Since claims are always arguable by definition, nothing anyone claims—even if it is strongly supported—will be universally true.

For example, if you research any given question about childcare, you will find several views that are based on solid evidence and reasoning (as well as a few baseless myths). Evidence and reasoning are the best guides in the absence of any other information. However, when you're solving a problem that is specific to you and your child, any argument that is meant to apply to as many people as possible may not apply to your specific situation. For example, if sleep is an exceptionally difficult issue for your child, much of the advice in popular sleep guides might not work for you. That doesn't mean those advice books are full of useless or wrong information.

Therefore, arguments that don't work in one particular case are not a reason to dismiss evidence as irrelevant in general, or to disdain a well-supported argument, since it probably still applies to other situations.

In short, evidence-based information is always better than no information or false information, but when an issue is dependent on individual circumstances, personal experience may be better still, especially when it is understood in light of whatever evidenced-based information most closely applies.

Arguing about Causes: Explaining the Past

Many of the arguments we see most often in the media attempt to explain major public events. This form of argument rests on causal reasoning, and it is a specialty of historians, who study change over time (what causes change, with what results, or "effects"). Think about the well-known example of a butterfly's wing having a ripple effect on large climactic events. When we're talking about the causes of historical events, we're looking at vastly more complex systems, since weather is just one tiny part of the entire universe of action and interaction.

Rules of Causal Reasoning

- The following rules of causal reasoning well-known to professional historians are all too frequently ignored in public discussions of what caused what. Keeping these rules in mind will make us better consumers of such analyses, and better able to reason our own way to causal explanations.

- There are always multiple causes. Don't expect any single causal explanation to explain every case, and don't stop looking for causes after you find the first one. Don't fight over what's "the" cause. Be suspicious of anyone who fails to acknowledge multiple causes for any but the simplest event. (For example, we can probably all admit now that Yoko Ono isn't the only reason the Beatles broke up.)

- There are always more than two sides, or ways of seeing an issue. The most useful answers are the ones that acknowledge that each person sees the world in their own way, and takes into account how those perspectives shape people's decisions. (The breakup of the Beatles looks very different from Paul's perspective or from John's, but each of their perspectives contributed to the event, and therefore neither is exclusively the "correct" one.)

- Some causes are necessary but not sufficient. Asking "if not for X, what would have been the same? what would have been different?" can help us think through the relative weight or decisiveness of any given causal factor. (Would the Beatles have broken up eventually even if John had never met Yoko? Asking the question this way forces us to look at all the other ways they were having problems, which is more useful than asking, "did Yoko break up the Beatles?" which discourages us from looking at other possibilities.)

- Don't confuse proximity to the event for cause. Some causes may have been a tipping point or trigger, but would not have had that power if not for other, more important causes that laid the groundwork. In other cases, what seems to be a triggering event could be just coincidence. (John Lennon's relationship with Yoko Ono preceded the Beatles' breakup and got blamed for it for many years. In retrospect, however, it is possible to see that divisions and difficulties within the Beatles may have enabled or encouraged John and the others to look to outside relationships. In this way you could even argue that the breakup of the Beatles caused John's relationship to Yoko.)

- Causal factors often function cumulatively. Something that by itself would never bring about the given result combines with other factors that also aren't enough in themselves, and all those factors together make a difference. (It seems unlikely that the Beatles would have broken up over the fact that they couldn't play live anymore because of screaming crowds, or just because of disagreements over management, or just because of band members' outside relationships. But all of those factors happening at the same time plausibly intensified the pressure of each.)

- Every causal factor has its power to bring about a change only in a specific context. You can't treat causal factors like weights on a scale that can be interchanged. Each factor is part of a continuous chain of cause and effect: each one arose in a specific set of circumstances, which have their own causes. (For example, we can't really determine whether the Beatles would have broken up in 1970 if John had met Yoko 5 years earlier, since the circumstances of the group, and John and Yoko's reasons for being interested in each other would all have been different then, in ways we can't guess at.)

- Don't confuse causal power with intent. Just because a person did X to make Y happen, doesn't mean X isn't the reason Z was the actual result. (When John Lennon started dating Yoko Ono, he almost certainly didn't do it just to annoy and alienate his bandmates, but that was part of the effect of their relationship.)

- Reasoning by counterfactual is when we imagine how things might have turned out differently if we could change one small factor. For example, "If John had never met Yoko, the Beatles would not have broken up" is a counterfactual statement. Counterfactual thinking can be a useful exercise because it pushes us to think through the multiple causes behind an event (what other problems would still have been there?). But we must remember that we can never actually know the answer to the counterfactual (that is, whether the breakup of the Beatles would actually have been delayed or prevented).

- Nothing is inevitable. Every possible cause depends to some degree on other factors. Never trust an argument that rests on the premise that once some event happened, subsequent changes were inevitable. Test it by imagining the alternative possibilities. (For example, one could say, "once Brian Epstein died, the Beatles could never hold it together," but the band's breakup was not a direct, much less inevitable, consequence of their manager's death years earlier. Imagine instead a path where the Beatles continued to play together like the Rolling Stones.)

Confusing Cause and Effect

Causes are the forces that push people to act in certain ways, while effects are reactions to or results of those events. Causes happen first, of course, and that should make them easy to distinguish, but it's not that simple when many causes are having many effects all at once. Our brains strive to make sense of each piece of information as it comes, and that can make us miss larger patterns, even simple chronological ones. In addition, our emotional responses to information can blind us to parts we don't like or care about.

For example, it is common to see a reaction you don't like (such as "people act like jerks on the internet") and assume that you are observing a cause ("people act like jerks because most people really are jerks") when there might be other, less obvious causes if we keep looking for them (people are confused and unsettled by the chaos of information on the internet, and also tempted to hide behind what seems like anonymity, and all this can result in people behaving worse than they would in a similar but face-to-face interaction).

Arguing about Effects: Predicting the Future

The other most common type of arguments we see in the media and on the internet are those that try to predict future events, or in other words, to guess what the effects or outcomes will be of a given event, policy, or action. When a talking head on the news or a journalist in an online magazine argues for a certain policy, or an activist organization recommends some specific action, they are making an argument about effects. An argument about effects is a kind of prediction about the future, but based on evidence and reasoning.

Arguments about effects are therefore fundamentally different from arguments about causality. They are educated guesses based on known evidence, rather than attempts to explain what has already happened. They are "what-if" arguments, logically based on the statement: "if ____, then ____."

For example, I could say, "I support a ban on ice cream because it's making us all fat." This is the same as saying, "IF we ban ice cream, THEN our population won't be as fat." This argument can be broken down into two claims: (1) that a ban on ice cream will result in everyone eating less ice cream, and (2) that eating less ice cream will result in people being less fat. In other words, I'm making a claim that these two effects (less eating of ice cream, and less weight gain) will be likely to result from the proposed action (banning ice cream).

To support those claims, I would need to show evidence that ice cream makes people fat, but also explain my reasoning that banning ice cream is likely to keep most people from actually eating ice cream. A strong argument would acknowledge that some people will make their own ice cream or buy it from illegal sources, and make further claims to address these problems, such as recommending a public information campaign about the dangers of ice cream and making a healthier alternative more available. This qualification and further claims are again based on reasoning about what the likely effects would be of each action.

Testing an Argument about Effects

The best kinds of what-if arguments are grounded specifically in what we know from the past about how things work, in what evidence is available about present circumstances, and in logically plausible predictions about the likelihood of events in the near future.

Ask the following questions to test the reliability of a what-if argument:

1. Is the information given about past events that have led up to or are similar to the predicted event accurate (that is, are they grounded in evidence that is corroborated elsewhere)? If you can't evaluate the evidence yourself, find out independently whether the most closely and thoroughly informed people on that subject agree on how to understand the lessons to be learned from these past events. (If a politician promises that there will be more jobs because the economy is improving, find out what the evidence actually says about the state of the economy. Since most of us don't have the specialized knowledge to make that assessment, we will have to rely at least partly on professional economists. Listen to several of them to find out whether there's a consensus.)

2. Is the information given about past events including everything that could be relevant? Is it a complete account of what is known? (For example, if you were to make an argument about today's counterculture by comparing it to the hippies of the 1960s and 70s, pointing to drug use and the desire to live more "naturally," you couldn't leave out the hippies' political activism and still have a reasonable argument, because that activism was a central part of the hippie identity.)

3. Are guesses being made about the future that are based on past patterns (that is, by analogy) very specific about what is, and is not, similar between the past and the circumstances leading to the predicted event? (If your boss promises that year-end bonuses will be as high as always, do you know whether he has looked at the relevant numbers to calculate that they are, in fact, similar to past years, or is he making a general statement of faith in the stability of the company? The former is more reliable than the latter.)

4. Does the argument cling so closely to past patterns as to suggest that the only possible future outcome is a repeat of the past? Our brains are wired to focus on the present, making only the present seem real and the future therefore feel unreal, as if

nothing will ever change. But change is actually the only thing that's inevitable. (For example, an argument that "young people don't vote" rests on the evidence that younger voters have not voted in high numbers in the past. But the voters who were young in the last election are older now, and there are new voters who may feel differently about politics. And what if the next election appeals to younger people in a way that no other recent election has? That past pattern could instantly become meaningless.)

5. Does the argument compare apples to apples in drawing comparisons between past or present and the predicted future? (The claim that "the economy will bounce back in 3-5 years" because that was the length of the previous economic recovery is assuming that the two economic downturns, and the responses to each, were essentially the same, and that outside circumstances are also still similar. Are all those assumptions warranted?)

6. Are there other, perhaps better scenarios from the past or present that could shed more light on the likely outcome of the event in question? (Pundits always like to predict how an election will go based on the past two or three elections that everyone remembers. But often a better analogy can be made with an election from a century or more ago if the circumstances are more closely comparable. See more on analogies below.)

7. If the future event being discussed is a deliberate plan created by some person or organization, does the argument consider not only the planner's stated intentions, but possible unstated intentions or unexpected outcomes? (For example, if a town mayor says roads will be repaved under budget, voters should find out whether a fair and ethical deal is being made to get such a good deal, and also what unexpected factors could increase the budget, like weather delays.)

8. Is the argument based on accurate and specific knowledge about the process or procedures in question? Does it take into account how things work, what is required, what the likely obstacles are, and what tools or strategies will be needed for success? Even the world's most talented person with the best

intentions is going to fail if they don't know how things work in this particular realm. (For example, a plan someone advocates for stopping the construction of an ugly new building should be based on what real, legal measures citizens have available to them, what people will need to do, such as researching zoning rules and filing complaints, and on what dates, in order to actually meet the goal.)

9. Does the argument acknowledge that the future is not, in fact, knowable? That new factors may come into play to affect the reasoning presented? What factors might those be? Anyone who swears that a future result is inevitable is lying, even if they present many convincing reasons, because nothing is inevitable. (For example, a critic could claim that a new film is going to be the biggest hit ever based on its many fantastic qualities. It may indeed have all those qualities, but no one can know whether people will really go out to see it until they do—or don't.)

10. Pay special attention to the difference between a promise and an evidence-based prediction. A promise simply says, "this will happen." You must believe it, or not, based on your trust in the speaker. Has the speaker earned such trust? Even a trustworthy person should provide evidence and reasoning if they are able, if they want your support, because you are an independent and rational being who should be expected to make an independent judgment. (For example, when one politician promises to never raise taxes and the other politician says he would try to avoid doing so but it could be necessary in certain circumstances, with examples and reasons, the second politician is the only one giving you a basis to judge him. All you can know about the first is that he started out by lying, since he can't know the future, and he didn't trust you enough to explain his evidence and reasoning.)

Arguing by Analogy

One of the most common, and trickiest, ways ordinary people try to argue about cause and effect is through analogy, especially historical analogies, so this particular method of arguing is worth looking at more closely.

Arguing by analogy is common in many academic fields and is probably more highly valued in fields other than history. One of the most famous analogies is Plato's analogy of the cave, which makes a philosophical and a political point. Scientists often reason by analogy, too, when they observe a phenomenon in one context and experiment to see whether it could apply in another, similar context. But these kinds of analogies are done by specialists working from detailed knowledge of both sides of the comparison.

The way we most often see analogies spelled out in general discussions are as historical analogies, where some well-known event in the past is used to make a case for where our future might go, or to explain how a recent event happened. It is interesting, then, that professional historians are often the last people to accept analogies as good reasoning.

This is probably because history is what we can call a "splitter" field, as opposed to many other fields that are primarily "lumpers." In other words, some scholars "lump" together a set of similar examples to find a pattern that can be used as a model to reason through new problems. Others, especially historians, prefer to focus on the differences between even very similar examples, "splitting" them and explaining why they are different. This is why when you make a casual historical analogy in front of a historian, she is likely to say, "no, that doesn't really work, because…." Historians hate to make predictions, and love to point out the differences between one context and another, because history is about explaining why and how specific events in the past occurred, rather than identifying models or patterns for future problem-solving.

While most ordinary people love to propose a good historical analogy, we equally love to knock them down, because "history doesn't repeat itself." But this popular pastime is based on a misunderstanding of how a good analogy works. When used properly, historical analogies are not predictions, and are not meant to suggest that history repeats itself. Historical analogies are useful only as a mental exercise of comparing and contrasting two situations point by point in order to jerk us out of our human tendency to experience the present as inevitable and unchanging. It is very difficult for us to imagine change clearly, so it can help to look at how changes have occurred before.

A Good, but Not Perfect, Match

The first key to doing a historical analogy well is to make specific comparisons between apples and apples. This is the main way that most attempts at analogy break down.

At the same time, you don't need, and can't have, a perfect match between the two halves of your analogy. No analogy ever can match on every point. But it's even more important to understand that we can learn from both the points of comparison and the points of contrast. The exercise is meant to help us see new factors and perspectives, not an attempt to find the most perfect match in order to earn brownie points.

Being Specific and Substantive

Each point of comparison or contrast in an analogy should be as specific and substantive as possible. A comparison like "both Jennifer Lawrence and Katharine Hepburn are female actresses who have worn pants in public" is vague, because there are many other female actresses who have worn pants who would fit the comparison equally well. This comparison is also not substantive, because even though wearing pants in certain situations was notable in Katharine Hepburn's day, but it not remarkable now, so there's nothing to be learned from this fact about Jennifer Lawrence.

A better analogy would be that "both Jennifer Lawrence and Katharine Hepburn are known for playing against girlish stereotypes by showing their enjoyment of sports and food, by speaking assertively, and by disdaining attention paid to their looks." This comparison raises substantive issues and provides several examples of specific similarities.

Of course, the comparison would be both more fair and more interesting if the several contrasts between these two actresses and their contexts were also pointed out, such as the fact that Hepburn was noted for her almost aristocratic manner while Lawrence is known for a raunchy sense of humor and blunt manners, not to mention the many differences between Hollywood's heyday and our present age of digital media.

Being Accurate and Comprehensive

For the past to be a useful guide in understanding causes and effects we have to be careful about which parts of a similar past event were actually bringing about the result we're interested in, and that we have considered as many relevant factors as possible.

For example, one could look at Barack Obama's election as president in 2008 and first notice the most unique aspect of that event: that he was the first African-American elected to that office. We are often distracted by personal characteristics, so it would be especially tempting to argue that Obama won because he was relatively young and charismatic as well as representing an outsider's point of view during a period of political cynicism and expanding civil rights. This would lead us to think that to be successful future candidates should be young, charismatic minorities. While those personal factors were probably part of the reason for Obama's victory, we have left out others, such as his innovative use of grassroots funding and social media, and the appeal of his message of bipartisan unity and hopeful problem-solving.

Analogies Are Not Exclusive

If one analogy is useful, that does not mean that other, completely unrelated comparisons are not equally useful in understanding the same event. You can compare a current event to several widely varied historical events and learn something different and useful from each. My analogy does not have to make yours void in order to work, and vice versa. There are probably as many interesting things to learn from comparing Jennifer Lawrence to Angelina Jolie as to Katharine Hepburn.

Comparing Public and Private

Analogies between public events and private affairs—though intended to make discussions of public affairs accessible for ordinary people who aren't experts in policy—often break down because of the problems described above.

For example, perhaps the most common analogy is to compare a government's economy to a family's household economy. But this analogy can't work, because no individual has the power to issue their own currency or bonds. That is a comparison between apples and oranges. Similarly, you can't compare a corporate budget to a household budget, when most households do not employ people or provide their benefits, and are subject to very different tax rules. A better analogy would be between one kind of business budget and another kind of business budget, or between one government's economy and another government's economy. There will still be points of contrast, but the most important structural factors that determine outcomes should be comparable.

The Only Constant Is Change

When you argue by analogy, you are using comparisons to help you find cause-and-effect relationships that are likely to happen again in a similar way. You're saying, since X led to Y in the past, X will lead to Y now. But since history does not repeat itself, and circumstances are never exactly identical between one event and another, there will always be factors we don't see or couldn't expect that can lead to a new outcome.

For example, let's say a given product, like Apple's first tablet-shaped computer, is very expensive, seems to lack conveniences that define competitive products (like a keyboard or disk drive) and has a really laughable name that makes it sound like a women's hygiene product: "iPad." It would be reasonable to compare it to previous products that were pricey, uncool, and had limited features and conclude that the iPad is likely to fail, as other products with those characteristics have failed. Experts, pundits, and the public could all agree that this product can never be anything more than a joke. But, if it turns out that that product actually has appeal no one had ever experienced before that makes the missing features unnecessary, that makes the price seem worth it, and that is so much fun we don't care what it's called, the same experts, pundits, and public will soon forget they were ever skeptical about this device, and compare it in hindsight only to previous products that broke new ground and succeeded.

Argument by analogy is, in short, not a way of predicting of the future (we can never know the future). It is a way of talking through the possibilities that is useful only so far as it is done responsibly and with an openness to the unexpected.

Conspiracy Theories

Conspiracy theories abound on the internet, yet almost no one would admit to believing or endorsing one. The theories we believe in are always the real ones, while those that only others believe can be dismissed as conspiracy theory. Our traitorous brains are very effective at bringing life to the stories we hear—this is how fiction works—but that's how even the silliest suggestion of a conspiracy can begin to seem plausible as our imaginations paint the words into a picture.

One of the interesting, and disturbing, effects of the information revolution is that we are seeing more widely accepted belief in conspiracy theories as well as a decreasing ability to distinguish between conspiracy theory and logical arguments about causation. This can perhaps be explained by how difficult it has become to distinguish between reliable and unreliable sources, made worse by an environment where we frequently feel stressed and overwhelmed.

Not all conspiracy theories are obvious. They are especially likely to sound like reasonable explanations when they're about a subject we don't know well, or worse a subject we think we know well thanks to Hollywood treatments. Conspiracy theories can be simple (such as the notion that the world is run by a secret committee of bankers) or complex, with whole libraries of minutely argued "evidence" (such as the many theories about the JFK assassination). Some conspiracy theories are an act of pure imagination, while others are closely based on truth, at least in part, but fall into conspiratorial thinking by assuming an overall design and malicious intent on the part of some person or group behind events.

Spotting a Conspiracy in the Wild

Resist the convenient notion that conspiracy theories are something only other people believe in. The following are red flags that suggest you may be encountering a conspiracy theory (any one of these may be explained away as a logical mistake or poor reasoning, but several of these signs together suggest a greater logical breakdown):

- Explanations of complicated events that give only one, simple

cause for the entire problem
- Explanations that require large numbers of people to think or act the same way
- Explanations that require large numbers of people to all share a prejudice that is obviously unfair
- Explanations that require large numbers of people to work together to hide something, and/or take personal risks
- Explanations that require many or complicated deceptions of large numbers of people
- Explanations that include an all-powerful leader or master criminal who is manipulating events

Conspiracy theories tend to come up in one of the following forms, which should always be looked on with skepticism:
- To explain a shocking, senseless event (the 9/11 attacks, the assassination of JFK, natural disasters, mass shootings)
- To offer a "real" motivation behind more easily explained policies that worry us (such as American fears of a Japanese economic "takeover" in the 1980s)
- "Alternative" popular explanations of scholarly ideas or concepts that have been misunderstood (such as paleoarcheology)
- Totally alternate visions of reality (in which we are all robots, or the earth is a game played by aliens, or germs don't exist)

How to Avoid Conspiratorial Thinking

There are several ways to undermine our natural temptation to fall into conspiratorial thinking. Ask yourself:
1. What would be required for the conspiracy to be true? Is it plausible that all those requirements could be met?
2. Do some parts of the "evidence" for conspiracy conflict with other parts? They can't all be true at the same time.
3. Most conspiracy theories rely on skepticism of coincidences (and popular fiction primes us to believe there's no such

thing as coincidence). In reality, though, coincidences happen occasionally. By itself, a coincidence is not inherently suspicious.

4. Conspiracies assume that people are all intentionally working together to create a certain result. Think about how the people around you really operate: most of us have a variety of intentions in different aspects of our lives and follow none of them consistently, while being oblivious to the intentions of those around us.

5. Some sophisticated theories suggest that people involved in a conspiracy are not consciously working together, but are all deluded into following the plan in the same way. While mass delusions certainly occur, they do not affect whole populations in the same ways and to the same degree. Look around you at any group of people you know well: how many of them think the same way about anything?

6. The goal of a conspiracy theory is always something nefarious. While people certainly behave badly all too often, how often do you see whole groups of people all behaving badly together in the same way, toward the same goal, with total commitment?

7. Conspiratorial thinking plays on irrational fears. Think through a rational assessment of the risk implied by the theory: is the theory overplaying what's really at stake, or the real likelihood of serious consequences?

8. "Occam's Razor" is a principle of problem-solving that states that "among competing hypotheses, the one with the fewest assumptions should be selected." How many assumptions do you have to make to believe the theory?

9. What parts of the theory are appealing to personal prejudices many of us hold against media, government, or other organizations? Remember that this appeal is part of what makes the conspiracy tempting, but it is not based on evidence, so it must be set aside.

10. What evidence or reasoning is not being considered by the theory? What else could we find out that could prove or disprove the theory? Where could that information be obtained?

11. Does the person or group behind the theory stand to gain anything from it (even if it's only the gratification of soothing a personal prejudice)? Are they doing their best to approach the question objectively, and transparently sharing those methods? Do they care more about finding the truth, or about being "right"?

12. A fun exercise that can help us think more clearly about conspiracies is to try to create our own and see how easy it is to come up with something surprisingly plausible. Invent a conspiracy by filling in the blanks in the statement: "_____ was caused by _____, because _____." Make up anything you think is funny or interesting. Now do a little googling and use your imagination to create a theory about how your statement could be true. Have fun, but don't post the result on the internet— people will believe it.

When a Conspiracy Theory is Just a Conspiracy

Actual conspiracies have, of course, occurred, like Watergate, the Dreyfus Affair, or the Gunpowder Plot, to name only a few of the most famous. Real conspiracies are notable, however, for involving small numbers of people, usually in direct contact with each other, who take risks that make sense in light of the concrete benefits they expect from the plot. Most real conspiracies also tend not to last long.

Conspiracy theories should also not be confused with theories that are simply false. For example, the notion of dinosaurs walking the earth alongside early humans is contradicted by every piece of relevant evidence we have and is therefore false. But it is only when people add the suggestion that academic paleontologists are supposedly suppressing data about dinosaurs living 10,000 years ago that the notion becomes a conspiracy theory, because it adds the element of malicious intent on the part of large numbers of unconnected or "deluded" people.

Propaganda

Propaganda is information that is spread to deliberately sway a person's opinion, especially in politics. It is usually used to refer especially to false information. Propaganda has been used as a political tool as long as there have been politics, but the mid-nineteenth century marks the rise of modern propaganda in Europe and the U.S., when popular representative governments, widespread discussion of public events and affairs, and mass media all made it possible for propaganda to reach large numbers of people and affect political outcomes. Modern propaganda targets whole populations, even sometimes foreign populations, rather than just small groups of political influential people. The significance of this development is that propaganda can now become part of the worldview of whole nations.

To accuse someone of spreading propaganda is an easy accusation, and most people misunderstand propaganda to refer only to lies our enemies tell us, rather than a tool nearly all governments and many organizations use, both for good or for ill.

Propaganda for a Good Cause?

Propaganda for a good cause is one way of describing what we usually think of as public service campaigns: efforts to accurately inform people about something they should do for their own good and that of the public, such as efforts to get people to brush their teeth and go to the dentist regularly, which have dramatically improved dental health in the U.S. in the twentieth century.

Propaganda can also be arguably necessary even when it is very one-sided or inaccurate, if it is put in the service of a good cause that is sufficiently important. See, for example, the anti-Nazi propaganda films produced by Hollywood during World War II.

The problem with this, of course, is that most propagandists probably believe they are lying for a good cause.

Knowing Propaganda When You See It

Common characteristics of propaganda include:

- Exhortations to respond with some action, such as donating, volunteering, voting, or otherwise supporting a cause
- An absence of serious discussion of evidence or reasoning behind the recommended action

- Emotional appeals (especially to anger, fear, and sympathy)
- Demonization of others (any effort to characterize people in opposition to the desired action as inferior, misled, or incapable)
- Promises that compliance will solve many problems, without explanations or concrete, specific promises

Resisting Propaganda

Intentionally misleading campaigns prey on our natural weaknesses. The only way to protect ourselves is to be more aware of how this manipulation operates.

1. Asking for evidence and reasoning, and getting independent confirmation of both, is always the best method of judging whether any statement is true.

2. We should also think carefully about why our source wants us to believe the statement in question. How are they hoping we will act on it? What benefit would that give to the source?

3. Our instincts tell us to pay attention to strong emotions, so we want to take a statement more seriously the more it makes us afraid or angry or sympathetic. But these instincts are wrong: the fact that a possibility scares us does not actually make that thing more likely to happen. If you read a horoscope that told you someone would offer you free cookies today, and another horoscope that told you are about to suffer a serious financial setback, your brain is perfectly capable of dismissing the horoscope about cookies even while it is likely to pause over the second horoscope, to think through what financial problems could possibly come up, and maybe decide to be extra careful, "just in case." This trick your brain plays on you can do real harm when it causes you to act based on false statements that were intentionally devised to manipulate this instinct.

4. Still another way that propaganda takes advantage of our natural weaknesses is to play on the illusory truth effect, where we are more likely to believe a statement if we hear it often, even if we know at the start that it is untrue. Try to limit your exposure to propaganda by ignoring such statements once you

identify them and ignoring sources that consistently produce
them.

Chapter Five

Reading Reviews and Advice

It is now possible to buy almost anything on the internet, but because we cannot see and touch products or talk to the sellers or service providers in person, it can be more difficult to avoid being cheated. On the other hand, shopping online usually gives us access to product or service reviews written by previous customers, and this information, if used wisely, can tell us even more than we would know from shopping in person.

The Art of the Review

The problem with product reviews, of course, is that most of them are meaningless. Some less reputable companies create their own fake reviews, but even if we assume a given set of reviews are real, many people mistakenly review something other than the product (such as customer service or shipping), confuse their own inability to read instructions with a fault in the product, review the category of things (chamomile's possible benefit as a health supplement) rather than the actual product (the quality of this brand of chamomile tea) or have far more precise requirements than most customers.

Finding the Good Ones

To use reviews effectively, you have to notice and discount those that aren't relevant. For that reason, looking at the average rating for a product is not very helpful, because you can't know what portion of those ratings are actually from irrelevant reviews. The only way to get real information from reviews, then, is to read the details.

Scroll through and look for keywords that indicate a useful review, such as comparisons to similar products, statements of having owned and used the product a long time, or explanations of how the product was tested or experimented with. One or two thorough reviews of that type are a better guide than a thousand reviews about shipping or statements like, "I just received it and it looks great!"

Tools for Sorting

Some sites, like Amazon.com, allow you to mark some reviews as "helpful" or "not helpful." The usefulness of reviews in general could be much improved if we all took the moment to mark the best and worst reviews accordingly, and to ask sellers who do not have this feature to implement it.

The best kinds of websites today have developed many such strategies to manage the huge quantity of useless information that fills the internet. This ranges from "helpful" ratings on reviews to forums that moderate postings and keep out unregistered "drive-by" users, to comment sections that use "upvoting" or thumbs-up/thumbs-down votes to make the more popular posts rise to the top so you can avoid the spam and trolls.

Professional Product Reviews

Still another way that the internet is learning to sort itself are companies that specialize in sorting data for us. The most useful of these are probably product review sites. Based on the concept of Consumer Reports—originally just a print magazine—there are now many other sites that have developed this idea further and many are free to access (they support themselves through links to the recommended products). Sweethome.com and Wirecutter.com do extensive testing of household and technology products, while also considering the products' customer reviews on the most popular sites. Still more specialized sites like TireRack.com, AutoTrader.com, and CarFax.com provide almost limitless information to shoppers in a particular category, like cars. Other specialized sites such as Ravelry.com offer a database, forums, shopping, and reviews for their particular niche range of products, in this case materials for fiber crafting.

Before defaulting to the common shopping sites like Amazon and relying on their internal reviews and other tools, try searching for terms like "reviews," "product testing," and "price comparison" along with the type of product you're interested in to see if better information is available.

Services, Too

A similar development is occurring with services available through the internet. Basic review sites like Yelp.com offer what are often real customer reviews, but require us to wade through many that are beside the point or too personal. Specialized sites for babysitting, home repair, tutoring and other common, locally sourced services tend to do a better job of vetting and helping you to connect with the right people, such as Care.com or SitterCity.com. Look for the ones you need through a general internet search with your location among the keywords, but also try searching Facebook, where many local groups find it simplest to organize themselves.

Advice

Two of the less commonly known sources of information on products—that are also potentially a source of misinformation—are blogs and podcasts. There are blogs and podcasts specializing in crafts, home decor and maintenance, DIY projects of all kinds, gardening, and much more. Many of the people running these sites or programs offer a great deal of first-hand, detailed information for free, usually earning only enough to keep going from ads or donations.

However, not all such sources are of equal quality, and the wise consumer will carefully examine a whole blog or podcast and its context before trusting the advice or products recommended on it.

Buzz Marketing

Since advertising companies are well aware that we are more likely to trust what sounds like an ordinary person recommending a product to us based on their personal experience, some companies create fake testimonials of this kind, while others hire ordinary people who have a built-in audience, like bloggers and podcasters, to sponsor their products.

The reputable way to do this is for a company to offer a blogger or podcaster a free trial of a product or service without any obligation to publish a review, positive or negative. The best bloggers and podcasters make a decision to either publish an honest review regardless of their opinion of the product, or to only publish if they truly had a positive experience. Content creators who are doing this properly will be open about it, so look for a statement about how they handle advertising.

If what you find instead are many ads or links to buy products without a disclosure explaining the site owner's relationship to these products, you should take any accompanying advice with a grain of salt.

Advice from the Makers

Sometimes advice or testimonials, often in blog form, are found on the websites of individuals or companies that are themselves makers of the product being discussed. There's no reason to assume these companies aren't being honest about their product, but you should confirm the information they offer by doing an independent search for reviews elsewhere.

Advice from Experts

Most blogs and podcasts will include an "about" section or first post explaining something about the content creator's background. This background should tell you the source of the creator's expertise on the subjects being covered.

For example, a blogger offering DIY cleaning solutions who has a chemistry degree is probably a safer person to listen to than one who doesn't, but since anyone can say they have a chemistry degree, you'll know for sure when the blog posts actually do explain how the chemistry of different cleaners works.

You can then independently confirm the essential accuracy of the information by looking up a few of the facts mentioned in another source, like Wikipedia (whenever you consult Wikipedia, take a second to notice whether there's a box at the top of the page noting any doubts or reservations about the reliability of the content for that page, and consult the edit tab to check whether recent, possibly nefarious, edits have been made to the page).

Clickbait Advice and Instructions

Beware especially of sites that offer advice or reviews that are spread out over many separate web pages, making you click a "next" button for each new piece of information. The purpose of this is to increase advertising revenues by making you click more pages.

Sometimes this is the model a site chose to make it sustainable for them to offer expensively produced information that couldn't otherwise be made available. However, most content creators of that type will offer you a way to pay a fee for their information upfront or are offer information that is valuable enough to attract more people and therefore more remunerative advertising that can be limited to only one or two pages.

Many click-bait sites that operate through these "slideshows" are probably not offering uniquely valuable information, and sometimes what they offer is just fake. Keep looking for a site that will answer your question without dragging you through the laborious and irritating game of clicking through dozens of pages.

Red Flags

Notice the language used alongside advice content on the internet. "sponsored content," for example, means someone paid money to put that content in front of you, hoping you'll buy something to make it worth it.

Always check the dimensions of a product and actually measure it out in space in front of you. Most of us are terrible at imagining the real size of an item from the picture.

Check for details about what is and is not included with your purchase. This information is usually placed in the smallest possible type and often requires you to scroll down.

Note also the kinds of sciencey-sounding language used to describe products that has no real basis, such as:

- "Clinically proven" (in what clinic, where? usually the company's own lab, without meaningful comparison to other products)
- "Made with" vs. "Made from" some desirable ingredient (how much of it? "with" could mean almost nothing, but "from" isn't

much better)

- "All-natural" (most poisons are natural…)

Similarly, notice small grammatical changes in standard phrases like whether a medication, supplement, or treatment "has not been proven to be effective" (which means we don't know yet whether it works—it hasn't been satisfactorily tested yet) or "has been proven not to be effective" (meaning it has been tested and we definitely know it does not work).

Limiting Choices

Part of what's especially difficult about shopping online is that we have such an overwhelming number of choices. Sometimes it's just not physically possible to consider every option, and even if it is possible, it may not be worth the time. Making some reasonable efforts to limit the choices can keep us sane and leave more time for more rewarding activities.

1. Prioritize the products and services you buy so that you spend more time thinking and researching major purchases like cars, appliances, or long-term services, and much less time on small items, where you don't lose much even if you miss a good deal. For smaller items, set an amount of time you will spend, or a number of options to compare, and stick to it.

2. Rather than comparing every possible variation on a product, first make a list of priorities. Do you care about color, size, functions, versatility, etc? Use the one or two factors most important to you to eliminate whole categories from what is available, so you can pay closer attention to the smaller number that are more likely to meet your needs.

3. The most useful kinds of shopping sites have filter functions in a sidebar so that you can limit your results to certain criteria, like availability in your size, price range, shipping options, etc. It's worth spending a little time to get to know how these options work and use them to get a list of solid choices rather than scroll endlessly through a larger set of options.

1. Another way to limit choices is to first ask your friends about what they like. Social media makes this very easy, and it also

gives you honest information and allows you to ask follow-up questions.

Chapter Six

Data and Statistics: What Are They Good For?

Nearly everyone enjoys citing numbers when they support their own position, but we are just as likely to become suddenly suspicious of statistics that contradict our worldview. Most of us are also aware by now that while the statistics themselves are objective, decisions about which data and what kinds of calculations to use are not. But since we often don't have the skills or access to verify these details ourselves, we can feel helpless. When this leads us to dismiss all data rather than sort through it to find the useful stuff, we're in trouble.

Numbers Are Not All the Same

First we must distinguish between data sets, statistics, surveys, polls, and deeper data analysis. These are all different ways of finding or using data with meaningful distinctions. Second, any of these kinds of data can be more or less useful depending on the methods used. We can learn a few rules of thumb to guide us toward better data most of the time.

Data sets are simply collections of information (a "database" is a large data set that you can search). When someone does some math to find patterns in that data (this is analysis), one of the results might be statistics, which are mathematical representations of the data, from a simple arithmetic mean to probabilities of how likely it is that a certain data pattern will hold. In casual usage, we often use the word "statistics" to refer both to the analyzing of numbers and the numerical results of that analysis.

Data can be gathered in many ways. Surveys and polls are two that we hear about a lot in the media, but data can come from scientifically conducted interviews, experimental results, or be reported by institutions such as police, hospitals or government bodies like the Census Bureau. Different methods are better for different purposes, and the scientific quality of any of them depends on how carefully the data is collected.

Deeper data analysis goes beyond conventional statistics, using data to understand connections between observed patterns, often in ways that can only be accomplished with huge data sets and tremendous computer power that can try out zillions of possibilities in the search for patterns.

Surveys and Polls

Probably the most common kind of data we see on the internet is the least reliable: informal surveys. We know not to take seriously the deliberately silly surveys about our favorite fictional characters or how our personalities may be reflected in cities around the world. But surveys that intend to show the relative popularity of people, policies, or other ideas that are based on internet clicks are not any better. They tell us only how many people in each group happened to come across the survey, while revealing nothing whatsoever about the actual question asked in the survey.

Sampling

Scientifically weighted surveys or polls, get around this first problem of how to reach a representative population by sampling. Good pollsters examine the characteristics of the population whose views they're interested in, and determine which kinds of people need to be asked in order to have everyone represented in close to the same proportions as they appear in the overall population. Then they either contact the desired people directly, or contact as many people as possible and mathematically weight the results of each group differently to make them match up to the correct proportions in the whole population.

The larger the sample, the more likely it is that the poll will be accurate. Sample size is about statistical uncertainty: if you toss a coin three times, you wouldn't be terribly surprised if it came up heads every time. But if you toss it 3,000 times, it is totally unreasonable to expect the coin to come up heads all 3,000 times. The larger sample is going to get you mathematically closer to a good prediction.

But the other difficulty is in the details of deciding what characteristics about people make them representative of others in the group. Voters are often divided by race or ethnicity, income level, gender, education level, party affiliation, and maybe one or two other characteristics. These categories are based on the fact that these characteristics have been found to be distinct enough to be reliable predictors of our votes in the past. However, all such calculations are based on assumptions that future elections will be similar to past elections. (Uncertainty based on having to make assumptions is called systematic uncertainty—such as when we assume that the coin we toss doesn't have the head on both sides!)

Margins of Error

Because this kind of data is based on assumptions and dependent on sample size, any analysis based on it includes an estimated "margin of error." The margin of error indicates that the predicted result could be slightly off in either direction, by some given numerical amount. One of the details you might find out from reading the fine print is whether a margin of error is accounting for uncertainty in the sample size, the assumptions, or both.

Sometimes an assumption turns out to be way off, and the poll turns out to be inaccurate. Such a result does not mean polling as a method doesn't work. Polls are statistical probabilities about an event that is inherently uncertain, so they will occasionally be wrong even when done as rigorously as possible. Such errors improve the accuracy of future polls of the same kind, since new information allows us to refine our assumptions in future.

Who Is Included?

One last factor that is considered when surveys or polls are taken scientifically is what overall population is being surveyed. For example, if election polls surveyed a sample based on the whole population of the United States, the results would probably be totally unlike the actual election results, since much of our population is not able to vote. Instead, sampling is based on either "registered voters" or "likely voters." Registered voters are those people who are able to vote, yet many, sometimes most of them, do not in fact do so.

Therefore polls based on registered voters may be inaccurate by giving too much weight to people who will not actually be participating in the election. On the other hand, samples based on "likely voters," in trying to avoid that kind of error, have to make assumptions on which kinds of people are more likely to actually vote, or express an intention to vote, in order to give them appropriate weight in the sample. This assumption is made based on past patterns, and it's a lot better than a random guess, but the extra layer of assumption increases the uncertainty of the results.

People Who Lie

And of course, people can lie when they are polled. Hopefully this is accounted for within the margin of error in a scientific poll, but that is not always made clear. Ideally the people running the poll know from how past polls compared to actual results what the likelihood is of lying or misleading results, in what categories and what rates, and they factor that into the math that analyzes the poll results. But because we may not behave the same way in the current election that we did in past elections, this assumption, too, can be a source of error.

Spotting Bad Surveys and Polls

When you hear surveys or polls discussed on TV news or in internet articles, your first question should be who conducted it, and what that source's interest is in the outcome. Some polls are conducted internally by a participating campaign, some are conducted by independent academic institutions, and some are conducted by news organizations with varying degrees of independence or scientific expertise.

Next you should ask whether the poll was scientifically conducted through sampling rather than just opened up to "viewer input" on a website.

Your third question should be how the poll choices were worded. In a legitimate, scientifically-conducted survey, questions must be composed neutrally, so as to avoid nudging respondents toward a particular answer, and so as to represent a full range of possible responses.

For example, a survey that asks, "what is your favorite flavor of ice cream?" should not have slanted response choices like "delicious mint chocolate chip," "plain vanilla," or "boring strawberry." And a survey asking "should our town pave its dirt roads?" should not have "yes, definitely," "yes, probably," or "I'm not sure" as its whole range of possible answers. The full range of answers should move from one extreme to its exact opposite: from yes to no, or from "strongly agree" or "strongly disagree," with options in-between.

Any report of a survey or poll that does not disclose who is sampled and the size of the sample, what questions were asked, what assumptions were made in calculating results, and the margin of error is probably not reporting a meaningful survey. Sometimes this information is in very small print or only available on the website, but it is worth seeking out if you want to know whether to take the results seriously.

Statistics about Uncertainty

Data analysis involves much more than gathering data scientifically, as complicated as that is. Statistics, for example, is one form of data analysis that uses mathematical principles to derive probabilities that one result is more likely than other results, and by how much.

Poll Aggregators

Thus, for political polls there are poll aggregators who use statistics to weigh a variety of polls, and often other data about the election, in order to come up with mathematical probabilities for certain outcomes. FiveThirtyEight.com has been the most famous of these since 2008, and has been the most accurate in three U.S. presidential elections so far. The site also explores statistics in a variety of other realms, from baseball to health, and includes explanations of the thinking behind their methods that are worth reading.

Understanding Probabilities

The first thing to understand about probabilities is that they are not predictions. Nate Silver, the founder of FiveThirtyEight, does not predict, like Nostradamus, a certain outcome in a given election. What he does say that mathematically, based on the available partial data, one outcome is more likely than another by a certain percentage.

Let's say he gives a 60% chance that Donald Duck will become the next Senator of Delaware. This means only that if the election were conducted 100 times, Donald Duck would win 60 times, but his opponent would win 40 times. Since the election is actually only conducted once, this is not a prediction that Donald Duck is going to win. Donald Duck is more likely to win, but not by a lot, and if his opponent wins, that does not "disprove" the analysis. The data was not wrong: the one trial that mattered happened to fall the less likely way. If the probability had been 95% that Donald Duck would win, that result is far more likely, but still not certain.

We also encounter probabilities in weather reports. If the forecast says there is a 90% chance of rain, bring your umbrella, but if the rain cloud gets blown off by a half mile and you stay dry, you are wrong to conclude that "weather prediction" is nonsense and you should stop listening to it. The forecast told you there was a 10% chance of the rain moving off, just as much as it "predicted" rain.

Accepting Uncertainty

The fact is that we cannot know the future. Our best analyses based on data from the past, weighted mathematically to account for what we know of the present, can still only lead to a balance of likelihoods. This is useful information when we need to decide whether it's worth carrying an umbrella, but there are never guarantees about any future event. We have to accept uncertainty.

Statistics about Reality

Other statistics we read about analyze past or current events, and are based on empirical data from what happened or is happening, rather than a weighted projection about what might happen. Where poll analysis is meant to give us an educated guess about the future grounded in what we know so far, other kinds of statistics are an empirical description of present reality.

Whether we are describing the present or projecting the future, the methods are the same. All statistics do reduce human behavior to numbers and use assumptions to guide the mathematical processing that identifies and weighs patterns, so they are never infallible, but empirical data and analyses of it are forms of real, not speculative information.

Stats versus Personal Experience

The greatest benefit of statistics is that they counter the human tendency to give extra weight to our own experiences or biases. When we encounter an event, our experience is also real information, but limited in a different way: we are unaware of all the other experiences of all the other people involved. What we experience may be representative—meaning it's a lot like what most other people experienced—or it may not. We can't know.

But rigorously gathered data from many of the people involved, whether it is qualitative (eye-witness reports, interviews, testimonials) or quantitative (numerical data on how many people did what), can fill in that gap.

Since our minds haven't developed to make decisions based on statistics, our gut instincts tend to push us to give extra weight to firsthand experience, despite its limits. Statistics offer a useful corrective, but only if we make the effort to understand what they offer.

Statistics are less accurate in explaining or predicting one individual's behavior, but they are far more effective than our own experiences in predicting or explaining the aggregate behavior of groups.

Judging Sources of Statistics

As always, the most reliable statistics will come from sources that disclose what data they gather, how they gather it, and the assumptions behind their analysis and the margin of error. Statistics are more reliable to the degree their sample sizes are large and assumptions are grounded in evidence and reasoning.

But any analysis can only be as good as the data that goes into it. The best sources of data are organizations that employ internal vetting, peer review, or other kinds of oversight, and that are not producing data for profit or because they are required to do so to maintain some benefit to themselves. That means that the most reliable producers of data are educational and governmental organizations or other non-profit institutions with transparent vetting processes.

Data based on self-reporting from for-profit companies is notoriously unreliable, and not surprisingly so, since such companies have a financial stake in getting a certain result (such as a cigarette company that funds a study on the health risks of smoking).

Applying Statistics

Remember that there is a very big difference between data and its analysis, on one hand, and applying it in various situations, on the other. A perfectly accurate statistical description of how students at a given school performed on a standardized test tells us only the range of performance of students in that school, which may be the result of many factors.

If we compare the results from one year and the next, we may think we can see improvement or decline, but we can't know that: we may also be seeing changes in the student population.

To know we are seeing improvement, we have to compare not the whole school's performance, but each individual student's performance from one year to the next. That yields more meaningful data, but still cannot tell us the causes of improvement or decline, since many factors, including student motivation, home life, nutrition, health, attendance, parental engagement, and school atmosphere have been shown to have dramatic effects on performance, in some cases more so than teaching methods.

Charts, Graphs, and Visualizations

We also need to be wary of how data is presented. Digital tools have made the process of turning data into visual representations much easier, and a good visualization can be a powerful tool for understanding. At the same time, charts and graphs can lend an impression of objectivity to information that is far from it. Charts are also made to be easy to read at a glance, and this encourages us to walk away with our first impression and skip looking for finer details.

As we have seen, the reliability of data depends on the details of how it was gathered and analyzed, so it is vital to read the fine print associated with any data visualization. We must also examine the proportions of graphical shapes to see if they really match the numerical proportions being presented. A bar graph showing small, medium, and big bars can show the difference between 1, 2, and 3, or between 1, 200, and 3,000: the second of those is much more dramatic than the former! Similarly, on charts with two axes, make sure the scales match what the chart is saying it will show, that a zero point is indicated, that all units are labeled and that the progression from one unit to the next is consistent.

Big Data

Today we hear a great deal about "big data." This refers to the enormous quantities of data made possible by the digitization of record-keeping in almost every sphere of life. Instead of using assumptions to identify a sample and then expensively gathering or weighting data from that sample, statisticians can, if given access to the digital files that now track much of what we do, actually analyze a full data set, such as every user on Twitter or every patient with spinal meningitis treated in a U.S. hospital in the last five years, or every traffic accident on a given highway over a set period of time, divided by accident type, damage, car makes, and other circumstances. Since so much of our lives is digitized, these enormous data sets can sometimes be connected, as when we combine traffic data with accident reports to draw conclusions about how to design intersections more safely.

Much of the benefit of "big data" is still potential, because all this information is owned or controlled by different entities, and comes in different, sometimes incompatible forms that are expensive to reconcile. Big Data also requires suitably enormous computer processing power to analyze.

And, of course, since this data comes from the footprints all of us leave when we move around in the world, there is an active debate about whether the potential benefits of analyzing big data outweigh the invasion of privacy involved in tracking everything we do and sharing that information. Responsible data analyzers should both anonymize their data (separate out and discard information that identifies individual people), and inform the public of what data is being used for what purposes.

Chapter Seven

Privacy and Security

One of the many confusing realities about our age of information is how it confuses public and private. We engage with the internet—that is, with nearly the whole world—from the intimate space of our homes or handheld devices. In addition, technology allows us to limit who we communicate with as much as it makes it possible to blast our thoughts to the world in an instant if we click a different button.

But because data is stored on servers outside of our own control (unless you run your own server with encryption), anything we do online has the potential to be made public by someone else, and this could happen at any time, since so much data can be stored relatively cheaply that we should assume anything we have put online will continue to be stored somewhere more or less forever.

At the same time, cheap surveillance cameras record our movements at intersections, tolls, and from people's dashboards and homes. That video can be saved, released at any time, and even combined with face recognition software (the accuracy of which is being improved by the tagging of pictures we all do on social media).

Explore the Wayback Machine at archive.org to see what the internet used to look like—and contemplate how little of what's there was expected to still be viewable by you now when it was first posted.

Controlling Your Information

A new fact of life of our digital age is that we must adjust to the reality of carefully controlling the privacy settings behind everything we do online, while also being aware that those controls may ultimately be meaningless.

- The safest assumption is that anything you put online or in "the cloud" through a storage account may be made public at any time. Consider this every time you put anything online.

- Make a backup of anything you want to keep on your own hard drive or flash storage, or in hard copy. Even though your data may be kept eternally somewhere, that doesn't mean you'll always have access to it.

- You should assume that public wifi is insecure. Don't type passwords or financial information while accessing the internet on such networks.

- Put your home wifi signal behind a password at a minimum, and the best encryption you can afford.

- Cover your webcam when you're not using it, to prevent hackers from accessing it remotely.

- Use strong, unique passwords that are not based on dictionary words. Better yet, use a password manager app.

- Never select the option to "show" a password, and do not save passwords on computers that might be used by others. Don't write down your passwords and leave them somewhere accessible to other people.

- When you enter personal or financial information on a website, check that the site is encrypted (there will be a small lock icon at the beginning of the URL in the address box and the beginning of the URL should be "https://" not "http://").

- When using social media, learn and use all the privacy options to limit who can see your posts. Make sure the parts of your profile that are public display photos or information that you don't mind everyone having.

- Look at your internet presence (social media profiles, forum posts, and any other content attached to your name) from the perspective of a future employer. Does this content reflect who you are in a way that is both accurate and professional? It doesn't matter if you're not seeking employment now. Someday you probably will, and those traces of you may still be out there.

- If you have children, think through how you want their presence reflected on the internet. Whether and how you post pictures and personal details, with what privacy settings, is a matter of personal comfort, but it's probably wise to think about it as much in advance as possible.

Managing Your Internet Identities

In the early days of the internet many people accessed it primarily under alternate identities, using invented usernames and avatars to stand in for real names and pictures. While this may have contributed to the often vicious nature of online conversations in those early days because people were hiding behind their anonymity, it also made online interactions often feel false or at least suspicious.

Today it is increasingly common for people to maintain a fully public profile on at least one social media network such as Facebook or LinkedIn with a real photograph and full name, though they may also maintain an anonymized persona for interacting in other online spaces, whether for privacy or safety or both. It is probably wise to think through a deliberate strategy of how you wish to present yourself to the world. If you want to maintain a private identity as well as your public profile, be sure to associate each with a different email address, and preferably even access each from a different device if you really need to keep them separate.

If the traces of you that come up first on a Google search are not what you would like, create a public profile on at least one major social media platform like LinkedIn or Facebook, and perhaps also on another site specific to your profession or interests. These profiles will usually rank higher in results than mentions of your name on forums or in publications.

Being Safe

The safest way to engage with others on the internet is to keep your own identifying details private and assume that the details you see about others may be false. But we can easily become overly paranoid— remember that it was common for nearly everyone to have their full name, address, and phone number published in the phone book long before the internet existed, and that most people on the internet, as in real life, are who they say they are.

Despite the dangers, it is possible to forge healthy, safe personal connections with others online. However, if the connection is real and respected by both parties, then neither should expect the other to be incautious. If you agree to meet someone from the internet, do so in a public place until you know as much about them as you do your "real-life" friends. Avoid sharing more identifying details than you would feel comfortable sharing with someone you just met at a party or your workplace. When first getting to know someone online, look for independent confirmation of what they've told you.

Warning Signs of "Grooming"

"Grooming" refers to the way manipulative people deliberately feed you what you want to hear and fulfill your highest expectations only to establish your trust. They pretend to have characteristics similar to yours, and to like the same things you like and value what you value. They flatter you and make you feel that no one else could understand you so well. After trust is established, they test boundaries gradually, asking you to do things you wouldn't normally do, which bonds you to them further, and makes you question your internal moral compass. They drive a wedge between you and your support systems so that you rely only on them. They "gaslight" you, pretending that totally untrue things are obvious to everyone else to make you feel like you're crazy or incompetent.

Anyone who engages in these behaviors should not be trusted. You don't have to believe the person is capable of perpetrating the worst kinds of abuses to admit that what they are already doing is unhealthy and that you shouldn't engage with it. The best way to combat these kinds of influences is to seek support and perspective on what really is normal from people who have already proven to be trustworthy.

If anyone you know becomes secretive and obsessive about an online friend, cutting off ties with real-life support at the same time, you have cause to be worried that that person may be involved with someone abusive.

For more information about online safety, consult internetsafety101.org.

Cyber Bullying

Digital media unfortunately has unprecedented power to intensify the effects of bullying and intimidation, by multiplying the ways threats can reach a person and by making them more public and therefore more humiliating. Forms of cyber bullying range from "piling on," when multiple users all heap the same questions, threats, or accusations against one user, amplifying their effect, to "doxxing," when someone's personal information is made public without their permission, to "revenge porn," when sexually explicit information that was shared privately during a relationship is made public after a breakup. Our society is just beginning to address this problem, but the following are some steps we can take if we find ourselves the victim of a cyber bullying attack.

- Young people who experience threats, intimidation, shaming, or other nasty communication from people online, whether publicly or through private messages, should let a responsible adult know about it immediately.

- The first response to such events is to document them: take a screen shot to record what was said and when, in its original context.

- Bullies seek attention and power. Find ways to deprive the bully of both: ignore and block communications from bullies and otherwise change your circumstances to minimize their power to affect you.

- Threats to a person's physical safety or doxxing with the intention to intimidate or make it possible for others to threaten a person's safety should be reported immediately to the victim's local police.

- Various services exist to help people whose personal information was made public without permission to "scrub" that data from the internet. Unfortunately, though, such efforts can't ever do the job completely, and can be expensive.

Spotting Scams and Hoaxes

On a much smaller scale, there are other ways scams and hoaxes take advantage of people all over the internet. Scam emails asking for your personal information are known as "phishing" scams. These emails can look very realistic, and often seem to come from PayPal or your credit card company or bank, asking for you to update your security or financial information. Most email applications will allow you to see the "full headers" that show where the email really originated. The originating address is often similar to, but not quite the same as the real website. Navigate independently to the real organization the email seems to come from to see if they actually report any security breaches, or contact customer service directly to ask if there's any real problem with your account.

One of the most common small scams are viral scares about Facebook privacy, in which people post a status update warning people of how Facebook is hiding changes to its privacy settings or suggesting that you share a statement that supposedly will protect your privacy from Facebook or other nefarious actors.

First, no Facebook status will ever offer you legal protection of that kind. Second, Facebook, like all the other sites, spells out how it handles privacy and security in its Terms of Use. This is written in legalese and is therefore difficult to understand, and its terms may not be reassuring, but they are there, publicly available.

The viral posts are just scams. When Facebook notifies you of changes, it won't be through viral posts by users. Official communications will come to you in ways ordinary users can't access.

"Raising Awareness"

Be suspicious of any viral status updates that pressure you to share. Even when they are not asking for money, or getting money from shares, these can be just malicious games to see how many dupes will unwittingly play along.

Some viral posts are harmless, some are fun, and some may even bring attention to a good cause. Raising awareness can do a lot of good (the viral "ice bucket challenge" did raise funds that led to real breakthroughs in understanding ALS!), but to be effective such viral messages should be saying something specific (not just "think of people with cancer") and be connected to a legitimate charity, where people's "awareness" can be channeled into real good through donations or volunteering.

To know whether a charity linked from an internet meme is legitimate, of course, you should do an independent search to determine whether the charity is as described and has a solid reputation for how it uses its funds. There are several sites that disclose public information about the financials and impacts of various charities, such as CharityNavigator.org, CharityWatch.org, and GiveWell.org.

Pyramid Schemes

Other viral status update schemes are essentially a new version of the pyramid schemes formerly operating through the mail. Any scheme that instructs you to send off something of value and promises that you will get more than you sent in return is an illegal pyramid scheme. However, many of these are passed around with the best of intentions, ask for items of small value, and with the explicit understanding that in the best case scenario each participant will get back only one item of equal value to what they put in (or not, if someone fails to live up to the plan). The safest way to participate in such schemes is to do so with people you are already connected to, and with clear expectations of what might or might not realistically happen.

Scare Tactics

Other malicious viral posts are intended to scare you, apparently giving the creators of the post a troll's thrill from provoking reactions and pointless paranoia.

When you see a viral story claiming someone was harmed in some shocking and horrifying way during ordinary activities ("Stabbed by a hypodermic needle hidden in a movie theater seat!" "Caught HIV from a public toilet seat!" "Robbed by a gas station attendant!"), remember first that when such freak crimes occur they are reported by legitimate news organizations, not through Facebook status updates.

As with other forms of fake news (see Chapter 2), do an independent search based on the location where the event is said to have occurred or the details of the crime to see if it was ever reported officially, or look for it on the various reputable sites that research hoaxes.

Remember that such crimes are incredibly rare, and when they do happen as a spree they are reported comprehensively in the locations where residents might have cause to worry.

Chapter Eight
Health and Science: What Will Kill Us This Week?

We have all experienced the frustration of hearing a news report—supposedly based on the latest scientific research—telling us that a certain food is terribly unhealthy, only to hear some time later another report—also supposedly based on the latest research—saying exactly the opposite.

There is so much of this contradictory and confusing information available today that the majority of us without the skills or access to evaluate the original research feel justified in throwing up our hands and dismissing scientific research as speculative.

There are also plenty of websites out there explicitly making the case that scientific research has been bought out by various entities, or that scientists change their minds and disagree so often, or are so often found to be wrong, that we can't really trust any conclusions. Even very reputable scientific sources themselves can be found in the media criticizing various aspects of peer review and scientific publications in a way that may make the whole thing seem worthless.

But science is still our best source of reliable information about the world around us. The difficulty is that science is incompetently reported by the press, misunderstood by the public, and undermined at its base by funding problems. These problems are surmountable, though, and part of the solution is for all of us to teach ourselves how to better understand science as we are exposed to it in our ordinary lives—and then support the funding of good science from independent sources.

What We Don't Know Is Killing Us

Most people manage to remember the steps of the "scientific method" that were drilled into us in elementary school (hypothesis —> testing and observation —> accept/revise/reject hypothesis). But (as an example of the Dunning-Kruger Effect) this small amount of knowledge gives us a false sense of confidence in knowing what science is about, so that when we hear something that seems absurd on the surface, we reject it without looking further and feel sure we are right to do so. However, that elementary-school level of knowledge is simplistic and partial, pushing us into false assumptions.

Science is a Process, Not an Answer

The first principle to understand about science is that it is a process of finding out information, not a set of final answers or a belief system. It is a common myth that science is the opposite of religion, for example, suggesting that one must choose one or the other view of the world. Science is a process of understanding observable reality. It makes no attempt to take the place of religion in offering explanations of what can't be understood through observation and measurement.

The Language of Science

The second principle to understand about science is that it has an internal language that uses common words in a much narrower way than they are used in ordinary speech. Misunderstanding key concepts is at the basis of most misunderstandings of science. The following are just some examples that are frequently a problem in discussions about science among non-scientists.

- Theory – In scientific contexts, a theory is not an idea or interpretation or a guess. It is the conclusion formed from the best, most thoroughly tested evidence we have. A scientific theory is the most reliable available explanation—the opposite of a guess.

- Climate versus Weather – Most of us refer to "climate" as "what the weather is usually like where I live" and "weather" as "how nice it is around me right now." But in scientific terms, weather refers to small-scale conditions like wind, temperature and precipitation, and climate refers to large patterns around the globe, like average global temperatures, wind patterns across whole continents, and so on.

- Average – in common usage, we think of "average" as meaning "common" or even "like me," since most of us think of ourselves as typical (one of our brain's ways of tricking us). But a scientific average is a precise mathematical concept. From where I live, it's been cold a lot lately, but that doesn't mean that global temperatures aren't higher than they've ever been before. We can know that for certain by mathematically averaging temperatures from all over the globe. A mathematical average is true even when not all, most, or even many examples from the given population have the average measure. For example, in a given population where most people are either quite short or quite tall, the average height will be in the middle, even if few or no people match that height. The average is still a useful thing to know if, for example, you want to see big changes over time. That whole population has gotten taller over time if the average height has risen, even though short people still exist and are still shorter than the tallest people were at that earlier stage.

- Chemicals – Most of us use the word "chemical" as shorthand for "processed substance that does not exist in nature." Many of us do also understand that in the scientific sense everything, including what we find in nature, has a chemical structure, and is therefore a "chemical." But we get into trouble by thinking we can leave what scientists mean by "chemicals" with them in their labs. We can needlessly scare ourselves into fearing basic substances that have been proven safe because of their name, and at the same time scientists' frustration over our hysteria and obsession with "natural" ingredients can make them unwilling to engage in public discussions of which fears may actually be worth studying further. If we want scientists to find out more about what is going into our bodies, we need to listen when they talk to us and engage with what they have already discovered, without being afraid of technical terms.

- Correlation / Association – When scientists say something is "correlated" or "associated" with something else, they are not leaping to the conclusion most of us do, that one of those two things causes the other. What scientists mean is that maybe one of those things causes the other, but maybe not. Further research is needed. It could be a completely random association, like the fact that the number of swimming pool drownings in the U.S. correlates with the number of films

Nicholas Cage was in between 1999 and 2009 (for this and other fun but totally meaningless correlations, see Spurious Correlations by Tyler Vigen, or the examples on his website, www.tylervigen.com). When a media report or blog says "science" claims something "causes" cancer, look for actual researchers behind this mysterious "science" and see whether they really use the term "cause."

- Risk – When we are told that a certain behavior increases the risk of some bad consequence, we often take this to mean that people who don't engage in that behavior are safe from the bad consequence, and that those who do engage in the behavior are doomed to the bad consequence. This can lead us to dismiss the risk altogether when we meet with one person who contradicts it, such as when we hear that breastfeeding decreases the risk of allergies, then meet a breastfed child with a severe allergy. Risk is a statistical assessment of probability (see Chapter 6), not a guaranteed prediction of what will or will not happen in each case. Similarly, if we are told that a certain factor increases the risk of lung cancer by 10%, people assume that this percentage is simply added on to our risk of getting lung cancer in the first place. If that were true, we'd all be dead, because the probabilities of all disease risks together would be well over 100%.

- Consensus – Ordinary people interpret "consensus" as "this is what most people are saying at the moment," which isn't an especially impressive notion. But a scholarly "consensus" means much more. Scholars have long training in independent thinking and their jobs depend on their ability to find holes and gaps in each other's work in order to improve on it. They spend years gathering evidence and continually re-assessing what it means with a conscious, deliberate effort to avoid agreeing about what it means. When nearly all scholars come to the same conclusion despite all of these factors fighting against it, they are making what is probably the strongest possible rational case that can be made for anything. There are, of course, examples of scientific consensus being revised or overturned (such as the continual updating of psychology's Diagnostic and Statistics Manual, now on its fifth major revision). Such examples can lead non-scientists to insist consensus doesn't mean much after all, but this is based on a misunderstanding of how science works. Because science is a process of gathering knowledge, not a belief system, instances of science correcting its own findings are the best possible sign that those findings are, in fact, reliable. They are a reliable reflection of the evidence known to us at this time. New evidence may emerge, of course, but until it does a scientific consensus is the best information possible. Thus, for example, our definition of "shell-shock," first observed in the wake of World War I, has developed into what we know call Post-Traumatic Stress Disorder. The change in name reflects a growth in our understanding of what it is, how it works, and how to treat it.

- Validity/Specificity/Sensitivity – In everyday speech we say something is "valid" if it's worthwhile or legitimate. Scientists sometimes use "valid" to mean simply that a result measures what it's supposed to measure (as opposed to results that are affected by other variables). More narrowly still, scientists use "specificity" to measure how often a negative test result is really showing the absence it's supposed to show, and "sensitivity" to measure the same thing for positive test results.

- Reliability/Reproducibility – The word "reliable" is used throughout this book to mean "something you can probably believe," but as used in science, a result is "reproducible" or "reliable" if the measurements are consistent in multiple tests.

- Truth – While scientific measurements are objective and scientific methods strive to eliminate bias, the results are still difficult to describe absolutely as "truth," especially when it comes to health and human behavior, since the objective facts of biology or anatomy that can be measured are affected differently by different individual people. As we have seen elsewhere, statistics tell us truths about a group, but as applied to individuals they are just part of the story.

- Proof – Similarly, researchers in any field rarely speak in terms of "proof" (that word is usually a clear sign that an amateur is speaking). Scientists speak in terms of "predictions," "associations," and "causal factors," not to be annoying, but to be precise about what they can say is definitely true, and what they can't. That makes their conclusions more reliable, not less.

- Nuclear – Having perhaps seen too many movies, most of us picture anything "nuclear" as freaky green radiation, as if it's a toxic gas or slime. The word really refers to anything having to do with subatomic particles, particularly the nucleus of an atom. There's nothing inherently dangerous or scary about the nucleus of an atom.

- Genes / Genetics / DNA – These, like other scientific terms, are sometimes taken to mean "synthetic" or "engineered," but genetics is the process by which all living things pass on traits. Genes are passed from parent to offspring, and contain DNA, which are like instructions to the body on how to develop. The word "mutant," especially, has been associated by Hollywood with aliens or even just strangeness, but scientifically a mutation is just a change that happens to DNA, including natural variations. Every cell naturally has DNA (genes) in it, and therefore everything we eat contains DNA.

When reading scientific sources, we should never assume common-sounding words are being used loosely, and we cannot rely on ordinary dictionary definitions to convey scientific understandings. Look up the most important words from a scientific text in a general encyclopedia or a science dictionary, like thesciencedictionary.com or thesciencedictionary.org.

Pay Attention to the Numbers

The third principle non-scientists should understand about science is that most scientific knowledge is based on mathematical proportions. For example, any given substance is usually harmful only after a certain amount, but the public usually hears only that the substance is or is not harmful, as if by its very nature.

No one can fully understand a scientific conclusion without first understanding on what scale, or to what degree, or in what amounts, the conclusion was found to apply. The difference made by an order of magnitude or a decimal point is literally the difference between life and death, sense and nonsense, rational caution and baseless fear. Pay attention to the numbers, and if they're beyond your experience, find someone qualified to explain them and follow at least the logic of their explanation as a guide to its reliability.

Science in the News

One of the biggest obstacles to the public understanding of science is science reporting. For-profit news organizations, or under-funded non-profit ones, are driven to provoke strong emotions that bring more eyeballs, clicks, and shares. So they dramatize scientific results to exaggerate any part that could be made to seem dangerous, exciting, or absurd, or they make positive study results seem like life-changing discoveries that apply far more broadly than the researchers actually claim, while leaving out the limits and qualifications all reputable scientists impose on their conclusions so that they reflect no more than what the evidence can show.

Another way media reports can distort how we understand science is by focusing on a few unrepresentative but dramatic cases, such as serious mental illnesses leading to violence (even though most people with serious mental illnesses pose more of a threat to themselves than to others). We are often left feeling more fear than we need to, while rarely hearing about other issues that should actually concern us but may be hard to explain or less emotionally compelling.

Mass media reports also frequently leave out the methods scientists use to test their conclusions, to mathematically weight how much their conclusions apply in given situations, and to account for other factors that might complicate their results. Without knowing these important reservations and how the results were achieved, it is no wonder that much of what we see looks ridiculous. What we are seeing is often so distorted that the true story is unrecognizable. For example, popular reporting on the risks associated with certain surgeries, or alcohol use, lead to contradictory and often alarming information that is almost impossible to apply to our individual lives, even though there is solid research behind these questions.

Find the Science Reporters

Some media sources report science much more competently than others. Look for outlets that already pass basic criteria for research and fact-checking (see Chapter 2), and then look to see whether they employ a dedicated science reporter with a science degree.

While such reporters are usually not active scientists and may have only a bachelor's degree in one scientific field, this background can qualify a good reporter to understand scientific terms and methods well enough to report them accurately and in plain language.

Such reporters are probably an ordinary person's best source, but you should still read them with a skeptical eye, looking for evidence and reasoning to support claims (see Chapter 4).

If you want to encourage the improvement of popular science education and reporting, consider supporting an organization like the Alan Alda Center for Communicating Science.

Find the Scientists

Outside of news organizations, some active scientists maintain blogs where they explain aspects of their work for a general audience, and comment on news items that relate to their field. Some of the best of these include Kristina Killgrove's Powered By Osteons blog, the collectively written Science-Based Medicine blog, the Blog on Math Blogs, PsyBlog and The Psychologist (thepsychologist.bps.org.uk). In addition, podcasts like Science Friday, Stuff You Should Know, and Stuff to Blow Your Mind can entertain us while also helping us to see how science research affects our everyday lives.

Spot the Quacks and Fakers

One of the best things you can do to keep from being conned by bad or fake science is to avoid blogs on scientific issues like health, food, nutrition, and the environment that are written by people with no science background, or with a science-related degree in a completely different field (such as a dentist writing about geology, or a geologist writing about oral hygiene, which is the equivalent of a car mechanic explaining a knitting technique or a master knitter telling you how to replace your transmission, because not all science is the same, to put it mildly).

When you see statements about science subjects written by nonscientists, look for their evidence and reasoning. It should be fully disclosed, and it should rest on experimental or observational results by qualified scientists in relevant fields, not on links to other blogs or websites. Reliable research can never be done through an open internet search (see Chapters 9 and 10).

Full write-ups of scientific research are usually only accessible through specialized databases or online repositories, and scientifically valid, reproducible experiments can rarely be run without professional training and facilities. Anyone who experiments at home or reasons from blog accounts is not really doing science, and is no more likely to stumble onto reliable results than anyone else who is simply guessing.

Personal Testimonials and Support

There's another form of science or health writing that is not scientific, but is also not quackery and can be quite useful in certain limited ways. Some people writing about medicine, health, or fitness describe their personal experiences without making any claims to having specialized knowledge, being representative of others' experiences, or giving advice. These kinds of accounts can be an invaluable source of support for people suffering from illness or working their way to better health. Writing about rare conditions, especially, or conditions that come with social and cultural dilemmas like stigmas, popular misunderstandings, or controversy, can help people think about these related issues and express their own experiences. The important thing to remember about such sources is simply that they cannot provide medical advice.

Reading Good Science

Even the worst kinds of reporting on science usually provide a link back to the source of whatever study they're talking about. Click those links and see how different the original report can be. Look for reservations and qualifications about how widely the results apply, and explanations of how the research was done, and what further research is underway. If you follow links back as far as they go and there is still no discussion of the methods behind the research, then you can probably safely dismiss a report as unreliable.

If you want to find out the latest research on some question yourself, there are some databases that the public can access beyond Google Scholar (which can be a useful starting point but is far from comprehensive). Try Science Direct, MedlinePlus, SafetyLit, ClinicalTrials.gov, PubMed and PubPsych (for health research), POPLINE (specific to population research and reproductive health), Science.gov (for government-sponsored research and data) and Science Accelerator (for government research on energy, specifically), ScienceOpen and WorldWideScience, TRID (for research on transportation), AGRIS and AGRICOLA (agricultural research), and the Catalog of U.S. Government Publications.

In addition, the Directory of Open Access Journals can point you to specific research periodicals on a huge variety of subjects, which makes for great browsing. Individual articles are sometimes made available by their authors on Academia.edu, through the universities that sponsored the research on institutional repositories, or on crowdsourced databases like Mendeley. To find the full text original research article behind a report you might read online, try one of these databases, do a general internet search using the name of at least one researcher, keywords of the subject matter, and the term "open access" (with the quotation marks), or search for a repository at the university where the research was conducted.

If you have university library privileges you may be able to access many more subscription databases such as the Cochrane Library (for reviews of medical research), Biological Abstracts, FSTA (Food, Science and Technology Abstracts), the Current Index to Statistics, and Academic Search Complete (which, despite its name, is not complete, but is a broad multidisciplinary research repository).

Another approach to becoming better informed about science research is to seek the long-form science reporting published in mainstream science magazines like National Geographic, Scientific American, Popular Science, Science News Magazine, Smithsonian Magazine, Discover, Popular Mechanics, Archeology Magazine, Astronomy, Sky & Telescope, Scientific American Mind, and Psychologies. Subscribing to these magazines is an excellent way to expose yourself to real scientific reasoning to counter the abundant misinformation available across the world wide web.

Finally, the private companies that host paid research databases make some research freely available periodically through, for example, the Elsevier, EBSCO, JSTOR and Cochrane Library websites or social media feeds, and this too is a good way to find out what real research looks like.

Qualitative versus Quantitative

Before evaluating any scholarly research, first find out whether the study is quantitative or qualitative, because each of those general types has different sets of rules for evaluating methods. Quantitative studies (as in "quantity," meaning numbers) rely on testing larger samples on a smaller number of variables, so that results can be as representative as possible. Qualitative studies (as in "qualities," like characteristics, not as in "high quality") usually look at much smaller sample sizes but ask many more questions.

Quantitative studies are usually recognized by the fact that results are explained in statistical terms. Quantitative data measures quantities, proportions, averages, percentages and trends. Qualitative studies use interviews, observations, small-scale surveys, focus groups and case studies as their evidence rather than numerical data, and can address questions relating to feelings, attitudes, impressions and conversations that are unreachable through quantitative methods.

Neither type of study is inherently better than the other, though each can be better at addressing a specific kind of question. Ideally, the two kinds of studies reinforce each other: knowing the details and context about individuals and small groups that we can get from a qualitative study can improve the way variables are identified and accounted for in a quantitative study, while the results of quantitative studies give us a sense of how much qualitative results may or may not apply in larger groups.

Evaluating the Strength of Studies

When you read about quantitative scientific studies, look for the criteria that determine how rigorous or applicable the results might be, such as:

- The study explains how it supersedes or adds to previous work on the subject, and explains the reasons for differences between this study and others.
- The sample size is statistically significant (generally, a large sample is desirable, though a fairly small sample can be

significant if the difference between the two test groups is very large, and some rare conditions don't lend themselves to large studies—a rule of thumb is 70 participants for each variable being tested.)

- The presence of a control. This is when the group being tested is compared to another group that is the same in every way except for the thing being tested, such as drug studies where one group gets the medication and the other receives a placebo, when both groups are statistically similar and treated the same way. Sometimes the control group receives the accepted standard of care rather than a placebo, though this has different implications for the statistical significance of results.

- It is "double-blind": neither the people running the test nor the test subjects know which group is the control and which is the experimental group. This is not always necessary, though, so its absence is not in itself a reason to reject a study, especially in non-clinical trials.

- The trial is randomized and/or controlling for factors that could complicate the results. The experiment is structured or results are weighted to isolate the effect of the experimental factor from other influences. The only way to know about these details is usually to read the original research, so be careful with press reports that may skip past these explanations in a way that implies they don't exist.

Ideal test conditions are not always possible, either because the ideal test would be unethical (often a problem with human and animal subjects—for example, it's difficult to study the effects of alcohol on pregnancy, since no one wants to encourage some pregnant women to drink in order to see what happens…), because it's impractical logistically, or because there isn't enough funding to follow through on a scale that would yield more conclusive results.

Find a Meta-Analysis or Review

One of the best ways an ordinary person can explore the state of scientific knowledge on a question is to look at a review of all the most relevant studies, called a meta-analysis or systematic review. Much of what is reported in the press may be too new for such analyses to be available, but when they do exist and you can access them, they are exceptionally helpful. Reviews summarize all that is known on a certain question, and usually offer a conclusion about the current state of knowledge without adding the reviewer's own interpretations. Meta-analyses combine data from many studies and do new statistical analysis on the larger dataset. Reviews and meta-analyses are written by people without a vested interest in the original studies, and they begin by selecting the soundest relevant research, so they can also be a reasonable guide to which studies are considered most rigorous and useful. Reviews from the Cochrane Library are the gold standard, and are partially available to the public at Cochrane.org.

Do Not Consult Dr. Google

One of the most directly dangerous ways we can be affected by misunderstandings of science is when we look to the internet for medical advice. Many of us feel forced to this last resort given the difficulties and delays of the medical insurance industry and the often very limited time we get to talk to our real-life doctors.

We know that "Dr. Google" is very likely to scare us with lists of common symptoms associated with horrific but rare illnesses, yet we often consult it anyway. The temptation is to believe that technology is making it possible for us to do deeper research on our particular concerns than a doctor can do, given her many patients. And indeed there are reputable databases providing accurate information on symptoms and treatment, like WebMD or the NIH Diseases Database, or NHS Choices in the UK.

However, what a doctor has that we don't is not just a medical school background that puts a lot of that information in their heads. A good doctor knows the symptoms that you can find on google, but she also has a working knowledge of medications, the systems of the body, and recent medical discoveries. In addition to this "book" knowledge, an experienced doctor has the practical knowledge of watching thousands of patients respond in various ways to various treatments, as well as long training in scientific methods of diagnosis and problem-solving. None of this can be replicated by visiting a website.

Of course, not all doctors are great at what they do (as in every profession) and even the best doctors can't solve every problem.

The medical profession is also prone to systemic obstacles like over-specialization, doctors not having enough time with each patient, and tendencies for certain categories of patient (especially women, minorities, and the poor) and certain illnesses (especially those associated with women) being taken less seriously. Bring your concerns to a qualified doctor and politely insist on hearing their evidence and reasoning for their conclusions. If they are unable or unwilling to explain their evidence and reasoning, try a different doctor until you find one who will, rather than turning to the internet.

Warning Signs for Health Advice

When you do see health advice online and are tempted to try it, at least ask the following questions before going ahead:

- Is the source of this information already known for sharing debunked or fake science? You can check on quackwatch.org, and if your source isn't there, search the key terms of the advice on DuckDuckGo.com to see if there are alternative views on the same subject.

- Does the person offering the advice explain their evidence and reasoning, and is it based on published, peer-reviewed scientific findings?

- Can the advice given cause harm? Remember that "natural" does not equal safe. Arsenic, hemlock, and foxglove are all naturally occurring poisons. Even "herbal" remedies have real effects on your body, but they are not regulated by the FDA for efficacy or safety. Homeopathic remedies probably do not contain enough active ingredients to have an effect, but for that reason are, as far as science can determine, a waste of money.

- Is the person giving the advice profiting directly or indirectly from what they are suggesting you should do?

- Have you already tried asking a qualified doctor about your problem? Can you bring the treatment suggestion you found to a doctor and ask not just whether she approves of it, but her reasoning for approving or rejecting it?

- If you're experiencing discomfort too mild or non-specific to bring to a doctor's attention, have you already tried common-sense healthy choices, such as regular mild exercise and balanced proportions of a variety of mostly unprocessed or lightly processed foods, while avoiding smoking and excessive alcohol or caffeine?

- Does the advice urge you to behaviors or a diet that involve the severe restriction, or excess, of any one nutrient or behavior? Such extremes should only be attempted with monitoring from a doctor.

The Statistics of Risk

One of the most difficult dilemmas many of us face in interpreting news about science and health is how to understand the statistics of risk. A statistic that a certain terrible condition is only likely to strike in one out of 10,000 cases is very reassuring, unless you happen to be that one case out of the 10,000. And if you or someone you know has had that experience of being the outlier, those kinds of statistics can come to seem meaningless. Once we reach that mindset of not knowing how to react to numerical expressions of risk, everything can seem scary—a paralyzing feeling.

As we have seen (see Chapter 6), empirical data has a great deal to tell us about whole populations that we should consider reliable information. Out of 10,000 people, if only 1 person really is likely to get terrible disease A, but 1,000 are at risk of getting less terrible condition B, this is real information. From an individual's perspective, however, there are many ways to think about how that information might, or might not, affect us. If there is nothing we can do to decrease our risk from either A or B, we are probably better off just not thinking about it (so turn off the TV). But let's assume there are potential preventative measures we can take. Our risk of getting terrible disease A is very small, but our risk of getting less terrible condition B is significant. To decide how we should think about this, we need to consider at least the cost to us personally of A versus B, and the cost to us personally of what we might be able to do to prevent falling victim to A versus B. Even though the likelihood of A happening is tiny, it might be worth it to an individual to take preventative steps if those steps are easy. Similarly, even though our risk of B is much higher, if the measures recommended to lower that risk are very disruptive to our current wellbeing, a rational individual might decide the risk is worth taking.

These kinds of calculations—making decisions based on assessments of risk, cost, and benefit—are actually the realm of economics, and some professional economists are publishing plain-language accounts of how to think through such problems, from the entertaining but less personally applicable Freakonomics to Expecting Better: How to Fight the Pregnancy Establishment with Facts by Emily Oster, who also applies these methods to other subjects in various mainstream media outlets.

However, be careful of applying economic risk assessments to health questions. Research on health decision-making shows that our real choices are actually reflective of a far wider range of factors than statistics of risk, such as motivation, perceived barriers, impacts on our social relationships, self-image, and others. Discussing your personal situation with health professionals and your loved ones is always the best way to understand the options and constraints that are specific to you.

Chapter Nine

Effective Searches: Google Is Not Your Mom

Most of us use the term "to google" to refer to conducting a basic internet search, even though there are actually a variety of search engines you can use for this besides Google.com. Most of us google things every day, but many people don't google effectively, or even realize that googling well means more than just typing your question into the search box. While you can type a plainly worded question just like you would ask your mom ("Where do I go to buy men's extra-wide shoes?") there are better ways to find what you're looking for.

Step One: Don't Use Google

The first thing to be aware of to improve your Google-fu (that's internet jargon for searching skills) is that each search engine has its own algorithm, or formula, to determine how to rank your results. Google.com not only puts ads at the top of your result screen, but it also ranks the real results according to the kinds of sites you have clicked on in previous searches (assuming you're using the same internet connection for most of your searching), or to highlight what it thinks will most closely answer your question. For example, if you search, "Does broccoli cause cancer?" Google will return results that say it does, even though those results are few and not well-supported. But if you type, "Is broccoli good for you?" the results will begin with many articles explaining how great broccoli is. Try it.

This is done to get you more efficiently where the computer thinks you want to go, but it also means you're being directed into a bubble of your own making. Depending on how you word your search, it can actually highlight misleading results, and even the best wording will only reinforce what you already know instead of bringing you new or contradictory information. This is true whether you're looking at politics or ideas for how to get rid of fruit flies or online retailers of wide men's shoes.

There are other search engines such as DuckDuckGo.com that

do not rank your results in this way. Choose it as the default search engine in your browser.

Step Two: Use Keywords

The next principle of good searching is to use keywords rather than whole questions, to choose your keywords wisely, and to try different combinations of keywords (which will help you learn what kinds of terms work most consistently).

For example, you could type "Can my landlord sue me for breaking my lease?" into the search box, and you will get some relevant results. But you are likely to get results that are more specific to your needs if you type, "tenant lease law litigation Chicago."

If you are searching for a person or organization with a common name, you can get better results by adding other identifying terms to your search. "Joe Williams" will yield too many results to sort through, but "Joe Williams Iowa accountant" will get more, though if it doesn't you could try "Joseph Williams Iowa accountant," "Joe Williams Iowa CPA," and combinations of the two.

Trying new combinations of keywords to get the result you want to come up on the first page is usually more efficient than scrolling through hundreds of pages of less targeted results.

Using Quotation Marks

Search engines find the words you entered in any order and whether or not they are near each other in the web site, but you can use quotation marks to narrow results for any words that should appear together. Searching for:

"Rebecca Jones" Iowa accountant

will find people named Rebecca Jones that have "Iowa" and "accountant" appear on the same web page, but searching for:

Rebecca Jones Iowa accountant

will find the Rebecca Joneses, and also pages that mention Susan Jones and Rebecca Smith, and so on.

Another important use for quotations is to make sure the search includes certain words that are normally skipped (called "stop words"), like a/an/the. To distinguish the satirical news site The Onion from the pungent vegetable, you would search for "the onion" with the quotation marks included.

Step Three: Stop Searching the Whole Internet

The third rule to good searching is to search a specific database whenever you can. General internet search engines like Google and DuckDuckGo search all indexed pages on the internet. If you're looking for common terms, that can yield way too many results. For some purposes, you'll get to what you want faster by searching directly on a site that has a specialized database.

For example, to find information about almost any English-language book, searching Amazon or Goodreads will get you to it faster than Google. Going straight to Yelp is a more efficient way to sort through reviews of businesses. Pinterest is a good place to search for craft, art, or other visual results because it makes browsing images very easy. But if you're looking for an obscure recipe, Google is your best bet since it can find it from anywhere on the internet, even while a large cooking site like AllRecipes.com is the fastest way to find and compare common recipes. If you want to know what people are saying and thinking about a current event, searching Twitter is more efficient than Google, and arguably more representative than Facebook (since many more people keep their Facebook posts private than on Twitter). If you want to learn how to do something, try YouTube, which is often much more helpful than sites like How.com or About.com (both of which can have more ads than substance).

Dictionaries and Encyclopedias

Most search engines now bring up dictionary and encyclopedia entries among the top results for searches on a single word, but you shouldn't just click on the first one you see. Dictionaries provide only definitions and pronunciation for everyday words as they are commonly used. Encyclopedias provide more extensive explanations of concepts that require context to understand, as well as basic background on people, places, and events. But some concepts are too specialized (or can have a very specialized meaning in addition to common meanings) for general encyclopedias like Wikipedia to be useful beyond the first step of identifying what a term is about.

There are some specialized encyclopedias on the internet, such as the Stanford Encyclopedia of Philosophy, though most require a subscription, like Oxford Art Online. You can find specialized online reference sources by first searching for a database. For example, search "database bra sizes fit" and you'll find the amazingly useful bratabase. com. There are also specialized dictionaries that give short explanations but focus on the meanings relevant for a certain field (like law), or on technical terms (as in science or engineering dictionaries). Specialized reference works providing more accurate and detailed explanations are worth seeking out even if that means locating a print edition.

So, for example, the quickest definition of a simple but obscure word like "louche" can be found on dictionary.com, but if you want to know what socialism is, or who Karl Marx was, your first stop should be Wikipedia (always checking for notices in a box at the top of the page about potentially biased or incomplete information provided by the editors). If you want to understand what existentialism is about, though, the Stanford Encyclopedia of Philosophy will tell you much more than Wikipedia can. If you're trying to compare the Adventist Church to related denominations, you should probably go to your library or buy the Encyclopedia of Christianity, or perhaps search Amazon for a historical overview of Christian denominations in the United States.

Finding Real Research Results

When you're looking for reliable information on any question where people disagree, you should of course first be aware that Google may hide information from you based on its algorithm. But generalized searches are also likely to give you too many results, filled with fluff that is either irrelevant or unreliable.

Many open-access academic databases relating to the sciences were mentioned in Chapter 8. Open-access databases covering other fields include RePEc or EconBiz (for economics research), ERIC (for education research), the Social Science Open Access Repository and Social Science Research Network (SSRN), as well as the Open Library of Humanities and the Digital Library of America. Ideally, you should go to your nearest library—a university library if you have access to one—and ask the nearest reference librarian about specialized databases for your research topic, as there are so many of them that professional advice can save you a lot of time in identifying the right source for your question. Library access may also allow you to search subscription databases like WorldCat (a catalog of books from libraries all over the world), Westlaw and LexisNexis (for legal research), EconLit (the database of the American Economic Association), or JSTOR and ProjectMuse (digital repositories for scholarly journals from many fields and disciplines).

If you don't have the time or access for specialized databases try adding the term "evidence-based" or "open-access research" to your general internet search. Of course, a website that uses those terms is not necessarily actually engaging in evidence-based or peer-reviewed work, so you still need to consider the nature and use of evidence you find there, but the term can help you narrow results.

Finally, scan the web addresses in the results to look for sites that end in .edu, .gov, or .org, depending on which of those is more likely to yield a useful result for your search. For example, if you want to know what your county recommends in flood conditions, search your county name, state and the word "flood," but scan the results to find an address ending in ".gov" to find official information more quickly. Similarly, a site described as an "academic commons" or research hub that ends in ".edu" is likely to be a repository for peer-reviewed research.

Chapter Ten
Getting Out of Your Bubble

Everybody lives in a bubble. We have to live in bubbles, both because nobody has access to everything all the time, and because we'd go insane if we did. Just the added information that internet connectivity gives us today is already driving us to the brink. There's nothing inherently wrong about your bubble. There's nothing wrong in having—in fact, it is healthy and necessary to have—a community or "tribe" where you feel you belong and you are especially loyal to and trusting of others. But to be a citizen of the world and to participate decently in a diverse, democratic society, you also need to acknowledge the bubbles you live in, and be realistic about their limits.

This Benefits You Most of All

Getting out of our bubbles is how we avoid falling victim to the Dunning-Kruger Effect, where knowing a small amount of information makes us see ourselves as expert and feel great certainty about our conclusions, when in fact there's a great deal we don't know, and some of that unknown information might be vital in making our decisions, but without knowing it's there, we don't look for it. The certainty we feel may even push us, without realizing it, to deny valid new information when it presents itself.

Bubble-Free Browsing

The first thing you can do to address this problem is to structure your world so that you get a view from outside your bubble more often. Change your default browser to DuckDuckGo or another search engine that does not rank results according to what it thinks you want. Curate a newsfeed or watch list for yourself so that you get news from a variety of reliable, professional news organizations, while avoiding known fakes (see Chapter 2 for places to start).

If there are people whose Facebook feeds you hide because you don't enjoy seeing their posts, pick a day every once in a while when you're in an open mood to deliberately go and read what's on their wall.

Perspectives beyond Status Updates

Choose entertainment that is made by people different from you: movies, TV shows, books and internet sites from different parts of the world, made by people whose lives and perspectives are different from yours. Fiction and history both encourage empathy and critical thinking by offering ways of seeing the world differently, by putting you in someone else's shoes.

The internet offers both free and paid courses and lectures on pretty much any subject in the world, often presented by credentialed, experienced experts. Look at iTunes university or Coursera for possibilities.

And, of course, getting off the internet and doing real-life activities, especially in ways that involve meeting new people or getting to know people better, will broaden your world. Even within your home community, there are social circles that will feel foreign to you, and you can seek them out.

Practice

1. The following are exercises you can do to remind yourself of what you don't know, and open your mind to new information that you may need.

2. Practice small talk with strangers, in real life and on the internet, by asking questions. Most of us interact with many kinds of people, but we rarely really exchange perspectives. Certain topics, like politics and religion, are considered impolite or too difficult, but if we never really communicate with each other, we will stay inside our bubbles despite personally interacting on occasion.

3. To broaden your horizons without feeling rude or aggressive with a stranger, ask open-ended questions and listen respectfully without trying to score your own points or defend your turf. If this is not something you're usually comfortable with, think of questions in advance, especially beyond the usual, "where do you live?" or "what do you do?" Try open-ended

questions that encourage longer answers, like "what do you like about where you live?" or "how did you get into your line of work?" Move gradually toward more adventurous questions like, "what's something that really bothers you about where you live?" or "what would you do with your life if money weren't an issue?"

4. Among people you already know, think about what friends or family members are expert in, and next time you have a chance, ask them about that expertise. Ask "what's the hardest thing about what you do?" or "what do you find most frustrating or rewarding?" Ask what is often misunderstood about what they do, or what motivates them to keep at it. Ask people about their hobbies, their favorite entertainments, and their life goals.

5. There are other exercises you can do in your head that will broaden your perspective. For example, if you think you absolutely know the answer to some question of politics, society, manners, or philosophy, just as an exercise brainstorm at least three other plausible explanations. Give it real effort, as if you're being graded on it. Do a little research to see what others have said. While this exercise will neither fully explain nor make other people's actions necessarily acceptable to you, it will help you both to develop empathy—which is a pleasanter, more positive way to get through your day—and to be honest with yourself about the inevitable limits of your own knowledge and perspective. Remember that there are always more than one or two causes of or ways of looking at a problem.

6. Another exercise is to choose some topic that you have strong opinions about, and make it a research project, as if you've been assigned it in school. Don't just do a general internet search: look at your local library's database and search Amazon for scholarly and journalistic books. Specifically seek out views that oppose your own, and read them in detail. You don't have to read all of what you find or do anything with the results, but make a good faith effort to find out how much thought and research exists on that subject, and how many different points of view are out there.

Getting off the Internet

In order to really get out of your bubble, reliably research any subject—or truly know anything—you eventually have to get off the internet. The internet is a miraculous thing that connects us at least as much as it divides us, and it brings us more information in our pockets than any human could acquire in a lifetime in any generation previous to ours. And most of that information is free. However, the truly difficult problems of our world cannot be solved in chat forums, and real research isn't about finding out what the pundits, or Pinterest, are saying. Research and hard-won, evidence-based expertise cost time and money, so they aren't likely to be given away on the internet. You get what you pay for with information as well as other things.

Learning Skills for Real

If you want to learn how to do something more complicated than changing a lock or folding a pop-up tent or grouting your tub, YouTube is going to quickly prove inadequate. Learning whole skills from the ground up—whether it's knitting, gardening, building your own computer, or mastering chess—is still best done from textbooks, reference manuals, or instructional videos that are compiled by experts and planned and edited to guide a reader or viewer through many steps and a great deal of background information. In many cases, taking in-person classes, where you can try out skills, get feedback, and try again, are still the best and possibly the only way to acquire new skills.

Real Research

Googling is not true "research." Real research is a slow process of examining and questioning what is known on a subject (not just what is online, but all of it!), gathering, testing, and interpreting new information, and bringing all that information together into new explanations and proposals, and then critically examining these, too. This is a process that requires huge investments of time and money.

Professional researchers are expensively trained—often for five to ten years after the bachelor's degree—even to be able to conduct such research, and expensive equipment or travel may also be necessary.

If you want to know what these kinds of experts say about

how to solve problems and understand conundrums, you have to read books and articles published by professional publishing houses that vet every word they release.

You can sometimes do this for free through libraries, and some of it electronically in your own home, but you'll have to access it not through Google, but through specialized databases (see above). But many such books and periodicals primarily sit on public library shelves waiting for you to hold them in your hands, the old-fashioned way.

Experts in Person

You can also get (mostly) reliable and interesting information by going to public lectures. These exist in many communities, often but not always sponsored by universities. Bookstores host talks by authors of both fiction and non-fiction on a variety of subjects. Going to a talk gives you a collective experience and allows you to meet people with similar interests but different points of view, and may also allow you to interact with experts in person.

Real Politics

Learning more about your community and government—and getting your voice heard—is most effectively done by attending local government meetings and town halls. Those who really care should even consider running for local office.

Going to College

The best way by far to acquire well-rounded critical thinking skills and specialist knowledge in at least one field is to enter a university degree program.

Some readers may have already been to college without having encountered what they recognize as an education in critical thinking. Some programs are very narrow and applied (meaning they teach more "how to" than "why"), and some institutions do not require the "general education" credits that are meant to broaden such an experience and ground it in critical thinking. Student cultures can also often demean such general education programs ("only the lame kids pay attention in required classes…"), and underfunded institutions often staff such programs with overburdened contingent faculty who are not paid to prepare, to grade, or to meet with students outside of class, and who have such heavy teaching loads that they cannot do their own research. Choose institutions that rely almost exclusively on full-time faculty if you can. If you can't, tell administrators about how their reliance on underpaid part-time faculty impacts your education.

Beware especially of for-profit institutions, some of which have been found to be fraudulent. Avoid taking on large student loans. Choose an accredited institution with the best reputation that will admit you and that you can afford without crippling loans.

If you have a good academic record, don't be afraid of applying to top private schools because of the price tag, because many of these offer so much financial aid that they can be more affordable to a competitive student than our currently underfunded public institutions.

Getting the most out of college is not just about choosing the right institution and showing up. College lasts (ideally) only a few years and is a unique opportunity to study both broadly and deeply with world-class expert practitioners in every field. Use that precious time wisely by focusing mindfully on the work and getting to know the faculty, visiting their office hours and asking questions.

Chapter Eleven

Too Much Information

Much of this book has been about wading through the low-quality information that floods the internet. Once you have narrowed your consumption down to higher-quality information, however, that still leaves a great deal to read and think about to even begin to understand many subjects, and most of us are already too busy to do that in our limited free time.

In addition, conquering the Dunning-Kruger Effect can be painful and overwhelming, because knowing how much we don't know can sometimes make us feel helpless or ashamed.

There are ways to make it easier, though. Professional researchers develop habits of sorting and ranking information to efficiently get through large quantities to find what they need. You too can become more efficient with practice.

Reading Efficiently

The first skill to develop is how to approach any text in a way that maximizes your understanding and efficiency.

Step One: Find the Structure

Before you dive in to read a text from beginning to end, step back to evaluate how it is organized, so you know where to find the most important parts.

- For books, study the table of contents—and the index if there is one—to see what is included, how the main idea is divided into parts, and where the most important ideas are explained (usually in an introduction, preface, and perhaps also, in more detail, in a conclusion). The first paragraph of each chapter and the first sentence of each paragraph usually point to what will follow, and the last paragraph of a chapter often includes a "takeaway" point or conclusion: these are the parts to skim to get an overall sense of the content.

- News articles tend to begin with the main details and fill in background from there.

- Opinion and persuasive essays tend to start with anecdotes and background information, stating the main purpose only toward the end of the introduction, which is often near the end of the first third of the whole text. The remainder of the essay will either lay out the case being made directly, or intersperse points of evidence and reasoning with further anecdotes.

- Scholarly research articles tend to be structured to make it easy to find the article's contribution to the broader discussion and the nature of their evidence, so that other scholars can quickly identify which articles are relevant for their research. In the hard sciences and related fields, each section is usually labeled, such as "methods," "discussion," "conclusions," and so on. In the humanities and social sciences the introduction will spell out the main question or problem, what's at stake, and the author's contribution, the body will discuss evidence, and the conclusion will re-state the author's claims in more specific terms and perhaps suggest future directions for research. Many scholarly journals in all disciplines include an "abstract" with every article that summarizes all the key points.

Step Two: Skip to the Crux

Before reading anything else, identify the following key pieces of information, which you should be able to find easily after examining the structure of the piece (with practice, this becomes very quick):

- Topic – What is the piece about? Titles and headlines are often misleading. The real topic is probably narrower and more nuanced than the headline.

- Motivation – What purpose does the piece serve? It is trying to raise or answer a question? Provide information? Convince you of a certain point of view? Offer a perspective? Sell you something?

- Point of View – What stance, area of expertise, or perspective is the author coming from? If they're answering a question, what is their answer? If they're trying to persuade, what is it they want you to be convinced of?

Step Three: What's Supporting the Crux

Scan through the body of the text to distinguish support for claims from other parts of the text like background stories. Read these supporting passages carefully, questioning all of it, especially when you agree with what is being written.

- Evidence – What evidence does the author offer to support claims, to explain, to convince? Look for examples, data, quotes from experts or witnesses, etc. Evaluate that evidence, asking where it comes from, how it is presented (is the author transparent and specific?), and whether it really says what the author thinks it says.

- Reasoning – Look at how the author explains the connections between the evidence and their own claims or explanations. Is that reasoning fully explained? Does it rely on logical fallacies or leaps? Ask what the author isn't saying that could be relevant.

- Hedges and Qualifiers – The strongest, most reliable claims should be hedged or qualified with words like, "in most cases" or "usually" or "depending on…." This is because almost no claim is 100% true 100% of the time. Authors who claim impossible levels of certainty are less reliable than those who are mindful of reasonable exceptions.

Step Four: Background (If You Need It)

What remains in the text is less essential, and if your goal is to eliminate some reading from your to-do pile, you may not need to read further. But if your goal is to use this text for some purpose of your own, you need to also consider the remainder, which can add nuance, color, or reinforcement to the passages you've already read.

- Narrative – Stories that fill in background, connect evidence to personal experiences to make it more accessible, or otherwise connect the dots may help to make a text easier to follow, but are not essential.

- Personal Details – Information on the background of the

author or key figures included in the text may help explain its motivation or point of view. Many general-interest essays provide extraneous details about the people involved—such as physical appearance or what their workplace or home looks like—to humanize or lend color to the text even when such details serve no other purpose.

- References and Links – Links or other references to outside sources are useful both for verifying the claims of the author and for seeking more information.

Information Management

The second most important skill to develop is a way of managing information so you can keep track of what you have learned and read and what you still want to know or find.

Notetaking and Organization Software

The same technology that has brought us more information than we can handle also offers new methods of managing it. The most difficult part about using software for organization and note-taking, however, is that there are so many options, many of them changing so often that we are forced to adapt to a new method just after we finally found one that works for us.

The differences between organization systems tend to be fairly small, and if we aren't too picky about details, it may be saner to just choose any established note-taking app and stick with it as long as possible. But the days of being able to simply use browser bookmarks and a desktop file system are probably over for many of us, if only because owning multiple devices is now commonplace.

The Key to Everything: Metadata

Even if you don't need sophisticated information management for your own files, you do need to have a basic understanding of how digital information is organized in order to understand the world around you. There is one key concept so central to information management that all digital citizens should be aware of it: metadata.

Metadata is the external information attached to a document, such as the filename, the dates it was created and modified, its format, size, the author, if it's a text, and technical details for images.

We all encounter one form of metadata all the time now: hashtags. When someone adds a hashtag ("#") followed immediately by a word or phrase with no spaces in a social media post, this enables other users to click on that hashtag term and be taken immediately to all the places it was used on that site. Although people often use hashtags for amusing commentary, it can be a useful tool for finding what interests you in the vast stream of non-stop social media chatter. For example, if we want to see all the pictures on Twitter of 2016's glorious harvest moon, searching "#harvestmoon2016 allows us to avoid other uses of the words "harvest" and "moon."

Other metadata can be added to digital files such as tags, categories, labels, and notes, which all add to our ability to find and sort information.

- Filenames are the names you assign to digital documents, plus the ending that designates the file type (like ".docx," ".jpeg," or ".pdf"). Many people enter the first thing that pops to mind as a filename, but putting a little thought into this step can save heartache. Naming a file "Lastname-Resume2016.docx" is better than "Resume.docx" because you will be able to distinguish it at a glance from later versions and if you share it it will not be confused with other people's documents. If you are making many changes to a document, save a new draft occasionally and number the versions, as in "SeniorThesis01.docx" followed by "SeniorThesis02.docx," etc, which is much safer and clearer than "Paper.docx."

- Tags are keywords related to the document (hashtags are an example of one kind of tag). When you tag many documents, each with at least a few keywords that summarize what they are about, you can then search this large group of documents using a tag word and instantly get exactly those documents you want and not others. This is often a more effective way to search than looking for the use of a keyword anywhere within a text, because searching through every word of every document takes longer, and can result in mistakes when words are used with slight variations or are so common that they appear in passing in almost every document.

- Categories and labels are also customizable bits of metadata that are meant to help you locate a desired document among many others. Usually each document will have one category and/or label, and several tags. So, for example, if you saved an article about a technique for knitting extra-stretchy ribbing along with many articles about crafting on a hard drive containing many articles on other subjects, the metadata for the article about ribbing might be "category: crafting, label: techniques, tags: knitting, ribbing, stretchy"

- Notes can also be added to documents in many management apps, so that you can add your own comments, or a note-to-self like, "compare this to _____" or "use this for _____."

Finding the Right App for You

To choose an app or desktop program for information management, first consider your needs. Do you save primarily text, or a variety of kinds of digital media? Do you need to save and share things across multiple devices? Will you want to share with other people? Do you want to be able to add a lot of metadata to your documents, or will a rougher system of categories and keyword searching be enough? Different apps specialize in one or other of these features, while some apps might be good at all of it but cost more money.

Sorting the Mess You Already Have

Coming up with a method of organizing your digital information is ideally done before you start gathering it: you can add metadata as you gather, and everything will in theory be easy to find again at need. But what do you do when you already have large amounts of unsorted digital information? Adding metadata and moving files can be incredibly time-consuming. The most efficient way to approach it is not to organize each piece in the order they currently appear. Instead, do a series of rough sorts.

For example, you could first roughly sort your computer files by broad categories like "home," "work," "school," etc. Then, separate "home" documents into "house," "car," "medical," "utilities," "budget," etc. Once you have relatively small groups sorted, you can add metadata like tags and categories to several at a time without being overwhelmed.

Chapter Twelve

How to Not Go Crazy

It is possible to stay connected and not lose our minds. But just reacting to each piece of information as it hits us—in the face of a digital tidal wave that never stops—is going to leave us battered and confused. Instead, we need to make an intentional plan about when and how we will handle information that allows us to maintain balance and respond to the information that matters to us with time for reason and reflection, while discarding what is misleading, destructive, or useless.

Being Wrong Sometimes

Even with a great deal of time and experience and strong information, anyone can get conned sometimes. The important thing is how we respond to such situations: digging our heads deeper into the sand solves nothing. Admitting a mistake and forging ahead is embarrassing in the short term, but ultimately leads to greater confidence. Do you want to know that your positions are based on objective reality? Or do you want to die on a hill that's ultimately built of shifting sand? New information should be welcomed, even when it forces you to alter a view you were certain about before. It is the only way to know you're actually right.

Making the smarter choice does not mean you have to drive yourself crazy spending a great deal of time you don't have researching every decision life presents. It doesn't mean you have to dwell on a negative view of the world. You can still use technology to curate your exposure to high-quality information to yield a balanced as well as an informed life.

Controlling Your Exposure

The first step is to become familiar with the settings on your mobile devices and on social media accounts you use. Just as you get to decide how you use social media, so does everyone else, so don't expect other people to filter what they do online to suit your needs. Take the responsibility of curating your own feed to meet your needs.

You can set your phone to block social media notifications or make them silent, and store the phone out of reach, so you have to get up to check it. This will keep you from feeling constantly bombarded, and allow you to choose times when you're already on an even keel to see what's happening on social media.

At the same time you can subscribe to local emergency, weather, or traffic alerts and set those to make an audible ringtone, so you don't need to worry about missing truly essential information.

Seeking the Good Stuff

If your chief social media exposure is often upsetting, try finding other feeds, like Instagram, Pinterest, or specialty social networks related to hobbies, to balance what you see.

Also try reading "The Philosopher's Mail" (thephilosophersmail.com), a light spoof of The Daily Mail tabloid newspaper that features thoughtful and positive content on how to approach media from a philosophical point of view, which was published throughout 2014 and is still available. Then explore the Book of Life (thebookoflife.org) by the same creators, which explores a whole range of issues with a long-form, contemplative, yet very accessible approach to bringing philosophy into your life.

Reining in Your Facebook Feed

Most people's main social media network is Facebook, and most people are frequently overwhelmed by negativity on their Facebook feeds. By making "lists" of your "friends," dividing them into categories such as close friends, family, colleagues, acquaintances, and so on, you can choose whose posts you read by clicking on any of those lists in the column on the left.

Alternatively, when you see posts that upset you, you can click the small down-arrow in the upper right corner of the post and click on "see less of this." Be aware, though, that this kind of editing puts you in a bubble, giving you a false sense of what ideas and views are really out there.

To counter the bubble without losing your mind, choose a time every so often when you feel up to it to deliberately check the feeds of lists or specific friends whose posts you have hidden.

Another route is to decide that you will use Facebook for positivity only and block whatever you don't like. Choose different ways to stay informed, such as regularly checking reliable news sites and Twitter, where you can also set lists of specific people so you can view their posts exclusively.

Controlling Who Sees You

You can also use Facebook "lists" to control who sees your posts. You have to first set your account so that only "friends" see your feed. Then, on each post, you can click the settings button and choose "custom" to exclude specific people or lists. This can allow you avoid drama and still share your thoughts and experiences with sympathetic friends. Again, though, this kind of editing creates a potentially dangerous bubble, and you can counteract that by occasionally posting a carefully worded post for all your friends, when you feel it makes the most sense and you are poised to civilly but honestly handle whatever responses come your way.

Escaping the TV

While the internet takes most of the blame for the overwhelming nature of media today, 24-hour cable news, the hyper-competitiveness of reality TV, and relentless TV advertising also take their toll. In this sense at least, the internet can offer refuge. Try using streaming internet media for entertainment and temporarily turning off or even permanently discarding your TV to give yourself more control over what you see and when. This control should be about avoiding pointless aggravation so that you can reach a place of calm from which to reach out for quality media that broadens your horizons, rather than about shutting yourself off from anything new.

Slowing Down and Checking Out

As a general rule, you can manage your exposure to digital media by both slowing down and checking out. Slow down by deliberately pausing before reacting to something you see online, and before you send or post a message of your own. Take care of a necessary task, take a walk or a shower, or help someone in your household to recalibrate your feelings and impulses before you return to your response.

Check out by taking a vacation from the internet for a set period, whether it's an hour or a week or something in-between. Don't just turn off your internet connection. Plan alternate activities: read, exercise, be outside, talk to people in person, use your hands to make something. If you don't already have a hobby that requires slowness, attention to detail over long periods of time, and tactile or fine-motor skills, try looking for one. These kinds of skills exercise different parts of our brains and bodies and encourage mindfulness.

Rules of Thumb

You can remember just a few, short rules of thumb that will guide you reliably in most situations that depend on processing information:

1. Ask questions
2. Follow the evidence
3. Confirm independently
4. Accept uncertainty
5. Keep feelings separate

We Can Do This

The information revolution has made the world a more hopeful place in the sense that we know much more about how to solve our problems than we ever have before. But in many areas we lack the ability to act on what we know, because the information is just so overwhelming and the chaos of so many voices is deafening. It is okay to tune out some of the time for our sanity, but we must also tune in with thoughtfulness and patience and willingness to learn.

###

Acknowledgments

The author heartily thanks Johanna Franklin, Sarah Beach, Alisa Beer, Liz Hayes, Rebecca Graber, Ashwini Jambhekar, Asher Kaboth, Colleen Flewellyn, Paola Banchero, ElizabethAnn Kelly, and Sergei Antonov for their thoughtful comments on portions of the manuscript, Sarah Roy for formatting the ebook and sharing her expertise on ebook editing and publishing, and Sharon Casteel for formatting the paperback and sharing her expertise on cover design and print publishing.

Whatever errors or omissions remain are of course the responsibility of the author.

The author also thanks Daniel Pickering for nudging her to do this, and Anya, Marina, and Sergei for putting up with yet another burden on our time.

About the Author

Katherine Pickering Antonova is an associate professor of modern European history at Queens College, City University of New York, where she teaches critical thinking through courses on historical writing, historical methods, and Russian and European history. She earned her B.A. at the University of Chicago and Ph.D. in history at Columbia University. She is the author of *An Ordinary Marriage: The World of a Gentry Family in Provincial Russia* (Oxford University Press, 2013) and is currently working on *A Student's Guide to Writing History* (Oxford University Press, forthcoming), as well as a monograph on the policing of religious faith in early nineteenth-century Russia. She blogs about academia, teaching, history, and Russia at kpantonova.com.

66033587R00078

Made in the USA
Lexington, KY
01 August 2017